THE GODDESS GUIDE TO BRANDING

Your Blueprint for Building
an Abundant & Authentic
Feminine Brand

JANE MCCARTHY & KATE MCANDREW

ILLUSTRATIONS BY LAEL NEALE

PEAKPOINT
PRESS

New York, New York

Peakpoint Press books may be purchased in bulk at special discounts for sales promotion, corporate gifts, fund-raising, or educational purposes. Special editions can also be created to specifications. For details, contact the Special Sales Department, Skyhorse Publishing, 307 West 36th Street, 11th Floor, New York, NY 10018 or info@skyhorsepublishing.com.

Peakpoint® and Peakpoint Press® are registered trademarks of Skyhorse Publishing, Inc.®, a Delaware corporation.

Visit our website at www.skyhorsepublishing.com.

10 9 8 7 6 5 4 3 2 1

Library of Congress Cataloging-in-Publication Data is available on file.

Cover design by Morgan Otto
Cover and interior art by Lael Neale
Interior design by Morgan Otto

Print ISBN: 978-1-951934-41-5
eBook ISBN: 978-1-5107-7876-4

Printed in China

For our mother, Jennie McCarthy

CONTENTS

FOREWORD   viii

1. A GODDESS TO GUIDE YOU   1

2. THE GODDESS INTERVIEWS   9

DIANA THE FREE   12
The Diana Interview
Yonder Cider with Caitlin Braam
The North Face with Sophie Bambuck

HESTIA THE SACRED   28
The Hestia Interview
EO Products with Susan Griffin-Black
Bobbie with Laura Modi

DEMETER THE LOVE   44
The Demeter Interview
Oracle Oil with Cristiana Sadigianis
Sway with Julia Marsh

MAIDEN PERSEPHONE THE DREAM   60
The Maiden Persephone Interview
Tea Drops with Sashee Chandran
Alice Mushrooms with Lindsay Goodstein and Charlotte Cruze

QUEEN PERSEPHONE THE FIRE   78
The Queen Persephone Interview
Sienna Sauce with Tyla-Simone Crayton
Billie with Georgina Gooley

HERA THE REGAL   96
The Hera Interview
Camp Wandawega with Tereasa Surratt

VENUS THE BEAUTY   108
The Venus Interview
Dame Products with Alexandra Fine
Baukunst with Kate McAndrew

ATHENA THE WISE   122
The Athena Interview
Ellevest with Sallie Krawcheck
Argent with Sali Christeson

3. YOUR BRAND BLUEPRINT   139

4. FINDING YOUR GODDESS   146
The Goddess Exercises
The Pressure Test

5. FINDING YOUR HEART   160
The Heart Exercises
The Pressure Test
The Heart Interview with Lori Boccato

6. FINDING YOUR GIFT   172
The Gift Exercises
The Pressure Test
The Gift Interview with Katie Conway

7. FINDING YOUR STYLE   186
The Style Exercises
The Pressure Test

THE STYLE INTERVIEWS   196
Symbols (and More) with Sarah Moffat
Color with Laura Guido-Clark
Voice with Myra El-Bayoumi
Worldbuilding with Ada Mayer
Digital Experience with Rachael Yaeger
Materiality with Lauryn Menard
Experience with Janet T. Planet
Sustainability with Nichole Rouillac and Vicci Baigrie
Community with Sarah Hardy
Culture with Elizabeth Barrutia
Abundance with Denise Beckles

8. BON VOYAGING   215

SUPPLEMENTAL   219
Fictional Case Study: Soft Scrubs Co.
Your Customer Toolbox
Design Brief
Notes on the Goddesses
Idea Orchard
Going Further
References

Branding is not only more fun with a goddess to guide you, it's also more powerful. In this book, we introduce you to eight ancient goddess archetypes whose timeless energies are alive in successful brands today. From there, we lead you on a journey to build your own brand in a way that is both authentic to your company and ultra-appealing to your community.

This is a create-your-own-brand book. A book for bootstrappers and for founders raising venture capital. It's also for business owners and leaders who are looking to amplify their company's presence. You don't need an MBA or a background in marketing to "get" it. Our method is intuitive and inspired.

Throughout, we're including interviews with founders who share what they've learned on their own brand-building journeys. We're also talking with branding experts who go deep with us on their specific disciplines of focus. You're going to receive a full briefing on branding from women who do this every day. And you will leave this book with a completed blueprint for your brand.

If you're starting your brand from scratch, this book is for you. If you're looking to enrich your existing brand, this book is for you. If you need to make a pivot and evolve your brand, this book is for you too.

Together we'll illuminate an abundant path forward for your brand, so your business can flourish and endure.

We're so pleased to be on this journey with you, and we're wildly excited about what you're about to create.

Cheers,
Jane & Kate

FOREWORD

Let's dive in!

FOR THE FEMALE FOUNDERS

A personal note from Kate

While Jane and I wrote this book for everybody who is building or growing a brand, I want to offer a personal message to the female founders out there and say: There's never been a better time in history for a woman to start a company. Technology has made it easier, faster, and cheaper than ever before to build the thing you're called to.

Whether you are starting an enterprise cybersecurity company or a neighborhood co-op preschool, the time is now to create new and better ways to serve our communities. And all of these businesses need a brand!

When women lead, extraordinary things happen. Over and over again, I have seen women not only build great companies, but I've also seen them transform how companies are built. Since the status quo was built neither by nor for us, inevitably our presence at the helm shifts the center. This is a good thing.

The new river of capitalism I want to travel on is abundant instead of extractive, collaborative instead of hierarchical, and flows toward the kind of future I want to live in. And it's not a dream. It's a vision that reflects the businesses I actually see women building. It's the world I step into when I enter the boardroom and the world I believe we can co-create together.

I want to be super clear: entrepreneurship is not for everyone, and you don't need to start a business to make an impact. Similarly, there is no one way to go on a company building journey. Sometimes you can (and should) quit your job to go all-in on your business idea. Sometimes it makes more sense to run a side hustle while you retain other employment. The systemic and structural elements of our society continue to make entrepreneurship unapproachable for many, and an even steeper hill to climb for women of color and transwomen.

There are, however, burgeoning ecosystems of support in this endeavor. More women than ever are in charge of investing capital and backing new companies they believe in. I am grateful to be one of these women and to spend most of my waking hours helping other women make their visions real.

I've been a venture capitalist for over a decade and have invested in more than one hundred companies. There's a lot of depressing data out there about how little venture funding women receive compared to men. And while it's important to sit with these numbers, I personally find my antidote in working with brilliant female founders, investors, and practitioners every day.

If you feel called to build a category defining company that shapes how we live, first, I want to tell you it is absolutely possible. I know this, because I've seen women do it and I'm excited to introduce you to a few of them in this book. Second, I want to hear from you. Reach out to me through my firm Baukunst. If you have a visionary idea with solid founder-market fit, I will enthusiastically receive your pitch.

Jane and I, and every woman participating in this book, want to see you succeed. We want you to make your contribution to the world we are all building together, project-by-project. So, whether you have a team or are flying solo, know that we are with you.

01
A GODDESS TO GUIDE YOU

BRAND
MAGNETISM

Picture yourself at a party in summer sipping a cool drink as the sun goes down. You look around the terrace to see who you'd like to talk with next. Suddenly someone catches your eye. She's luminous. You've never met her before, but you sense an instant connection. Excited, you walk over and introduce yourself. As the two of you chat, your intuition is confirmed. You get a wonderful feeling just being around her. A friendship begins to bloom . . .

Branding is about giving your business this kind of magnetic presence. The kind of charisma that catches people's attention at a party and draws them toward you. From there, it's about making such a good impression that people not only remember who you are but want you to be part of their lives moving forward.

What gives people this kind of magnetic presence?

First, they're authentic. They're fully themselves. They're not trying to be like anyone else and so, they're unique. They stand out from the crowd and often are considered real characters.

They're also passionate. They live from the heart and follow where their heart leads them. This creates a questing energy that's highly attractive.

Finally, they make a positive impact on everyone around them. People enjoy spending time with them and like how they feel afterward.

It's the same with brands. Brands who are authentic, who are passionate, and who make a positive impact are magnetic.

The aim of this book is to get your brand to this place where you're attracting your desired customers and forming a bond with them that will reap exponential rewards. The key to getting there? An archetypal goddess to guide and inspire you.

Archetypes are the essential universal thought forms available to human consciousness during all periods of time.

Demetra George and Douglas Bloch
Asteroid Goddesses

WHAT MAKES AN ARCHETYPE?

An archetype is a character who is deeply familiar to us. The kind of character who has existed throughout time—as relevant to Shakespeare as she is to us now. Though she wears different costumes, her essence remains the same century after century.

An archetype is not an actual person, but rather personifies a particular energy or quality that is essential to the human experience. We all naturally relate to this character. We connect with her and feel we know and understand her. And we do. The archetypes are outward expressions of qualities that live inside all of us, within our own hearts.

HOLLYWOOD ARCHETYPES

In the past century, few things have been more magnetic than the films of Hollywood. Hollywood has mesmerized and enchanted us. It has also transformed actors, flesh and blood humans, into immortal icons. What is Hollywood entertainment made of? Archetypes. Archetypal characters are the stuff of Hollywood stardust. They are the essential ingredients for storytelling on a grand scale. The clowns of comedies. The heroes of science fiction. The outlaws of westerns. We get these characters. We feel we know and understand them.

Even if we ourselves have never downed a whiskey in a saloon while the corrupt sheriff waits outside polishing his pistol, we still resonate with the energy of the outlaw. Because

Where stereotypes are like cartoons that offer a simplistic experience, archetypes are more like poems that add depth and richness to experience.

Margaret Pott Hartwell and Joshua C. Chen
Archetypes In Branding

somewhere in each of us, there's a rebel streak. And this resonance, this sense of deep familiarity, creates an instant connection with that character. We care about them and want to know what happens next.

BRAND ARCHETYPES

Iconic brands are also inspired by archetypal characters. These brands channel the energy of their chosen archetype to powerful affect. When you invite an archetype to guide and inspire your brand, this timeless character connects you to ideas and emotions that are much larger than the material function of your company's products and services. Your brand begins to take on the special energy your archetype represents.

In a sense your brand becomes this character for your customers. This is magnetic. People embrace the emotions and ideas your brand conjures in them. They start to bond with you.

BULLSEYE BRAND TRANSMISSIONS

We like to call quick, high impact communications bullseye brand transmissions. Bullseye brand transmissions are clear, they're direct, and they fly straight to the hearts of your customers.

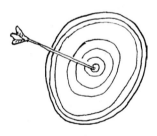

Your archetype can help you craft this kind of communication because she speaks a universal language—the language of symbol and story. She will lead you to words, phrases, colors, and images that are packed with meaning. This is heart and soul language. It resonates with customers and evokes strong emotion. It also tells them a whole lot about who you are as a brand in a very short amount of time.

In today's hyper-stimulating media environment, this kind of shorthand is important. You need to be able to connect with people in a blink.

Because archetypal images are part of our collective human inheritance; they are "familiar." Myths from Greece that go back over 3,000 years stay alive, are told and retold, because the gods and goddesses speak to us truths of human nature.

Jean Shinoda Bolen
Gods in Everyman

CALLING ON THE GODDESS

There are many ways to define the archetypal characters who have been meaningful to humanity throughout time. In our brand-building journey together, we're calling on the goddess.

Though their myths were written thousands of years ago, the goddesses are still very much alive in our collective imagination today. They continue to attract and fascinate us. Wonder Woman, for example, is a contemporary expression of the ancient goddess Diana. As is Katniss Everdeen of *Hunger Games* fame.

What's especially useful about the goddess archetypes is they transcend the kind of paper-thin stereotypes that dominated marketing for so long. Instead, the goddesses offer lush, layered images and messages that are genuinely inspiring.

They inspire us because they remind us of the grace, the beauty, and the power that lives within each of us. We all like to be reminded, and perhaps even need to be reminded, of the immaculate qualities inherent to our own natures. The goddess does this for us. She helps us cultivate and unfold the experiences that are our birthright to know and to enjoy. And so, she endures.

Brands who align with the archetypal energy of the goddess and therefore, speak to the rich firmament of the human experience ... Brands who tell the truth, instead of fool ... Brands who inspire, instead of instigate an impossible aspiration cycle that always bottoms out in dissatisfaction, can—and do—thrive in our current environment.

We'll meet some of these brands, along with their founders, in the next chapter.

Why The Goddess?

A personal note from Jane

Traditionally, marketers have relied on Carl Jung's set of twelve essential archetypes to develop iconic brand identities. Throughout my career in advertising, I have used Jung's "Big Twelve" countless times and experienced firsthand the power of these characters in the brand-building process. However, I've felt something was lacking when it came to building a brand with a more feminine identity.

During one memorable branding workshop, I found myself standing in a large boardroom at a major multinational corporation looking out over the city. Pasted on the window was a profile of "The Seductress" (a spin on the "The Lover") that the company's marketing team had developed. The graphic on the poster showed a Betty Boop style cartoon woman wearing a short dress and high heels. She had a martini glass in one hand and lipstick in the other. I was bummed. I looked around the room and thought, *There are good people here who want to do good work, but I'm not sure we can get to good work when this is our source material.* I felt sure there was a better way but didn't yet know what that was.

About a year later, I had a lightning flash moment when I discovered Jungian analyst Jean Shinoda Bolen's seminal book *Goddesses in Everywoman.* Bolen utilized the ancient Greek goddess system to evoke the universal archetypes through the female lens. I found Bolen's work fascinating. It offered so much more depth than anything I'd previously encountered about archetypes. I decided to use her work as a foundation for developing goddess archetypes for branding, layering Bolen's wisdom with insights from my own study of the Enneagram, archetypal astrology, and mythology. This blend became the goddess system we share in the book.

Kate and I both went into this project with our own personal, "favorite" goddesses, a bias probably formed as children pouring over our family's copy of *D'Aulaires' Book of Greek Myths.* With its wild, luminous drawings, the book always seemed to glow from the shelf. We gorged on its sumptuousness and took its myths at face value. In creating this book, we began to view the goddesses, and their myths, in a new light. We let our favoritism drop away and came to see how each goddess has a distinct grace and a deep power. We fell in love with all of them.

When working with an archetype, you are channeling a powerful force. There's a responsibility that comes with that. In our interpretations of some of the goddesses, we have made conscious choices about what aspects of the mythology to focus on and what to let fall by the wayside. Our aim has been to offer the highest, lightest interpretations we can. In these cases, we've included background notes on our characterization of the goddess. These notes can be found at the back of the book.

You'll see that we use both Greek and Roman names. For each goddess, we chose the name that felt most powerful within the contemporary context. For instance, we believe "Diana" sounds more relevant than "Artemis" today and so, we went with Diana.

As Carl Jung illumines, the archetypal forces are universal the world over. They are common to the "collective unconscious." However, how they are expressed is unique and special to each tradition and cosmology.

While we are focusing on the Greco-Roman goddesses, for each, we share a constellation of archetypally related goddesses from across the world and across time who might also be inspiring.

Given the need for richer, deeper interpretations of the archetypal feminine within the marketing canon, along with our own personal passion, this book emphasizes the goddesses, but the gods are also present. As you meet each goddess, we also introduce you to her counterpart—the god who represents a complementary archetypal energy. Feminine/masculine energetics are fluid. In branding, as in life, they intermingle. And so, we think you'll find that the gods add a breadth to the system shared here.

The best brands embody mythic archetypes. They literally are stories. Nike is a great example. Nike calls on the goddess. She is not the goddess of sport, or sportsmanship, or of fair play, or achievement. Nike is the goddess of victory.

Brian Collins in *Brand Thinking and Other Noble Pursuits* by Debbie Millman

A NEW HIRE

The bottom line—you're about to make a new hire. You'll be adding a new team member to your company roster. The open position? Brand Goddess.

Your goddess will inspire your whole brand creation process. She'll give you all kinds of ideas for how to create a brand that's authentic, appealing, and impactful. In other words, she'll help you create a brand that's mega-magnetic.

The question is—who is the right goddess for you? To answer this, we first need to meet and get to know these archetypes.

Once you're acquainted with the goddesses, we're going to lead you through a series of exercises to help you choose the right archetype for your brand. From there, we'll help you build the rest of your brand blueprint including finding your heart (what matters most to you), your gift (the positive experience you intend to give people), and your style (how you show up in the world). Your completed blueprint will serve as the foundational strategy for your brand, informing everything you do from here on out. For now, let's meet the goddesses!

02
THE GODDESS
INTERVIEWS

W e're now going to interview each archetypal goddess. As we do, allow yourself a minute to imagine how she might influence the direction of your brand, given her special qualities and the gifts she has to offer. We encourage you to keep an open mind here. An unexpected goddess can often make a strong hire. The interview format we're using:

THE GODDESS INTERVIEWS

In a nutshell, who are you?
Her simple, quick bio.

What's in your heart?
What matters most to her.

What gifts do you bring?
The positive impact she can make in customers' lives.

What's your style?
The attitude, words, symbols, and colors
associated with her.

Who are your favorite icons?
Cultural figures and fictional characters
she resonates with.

Who is in your constellation?

Goddesses from around the world and throughout time
who she relates to.

Who is your counterpart?

The god who represents the same essential archetypal
energy, expressing it through a complementary lens.

After each interview, we show how the energy of the goddess is alive in successful brands today. We also speak with
founders of brands that play in this same archetypal space.

The goddess is in the office.

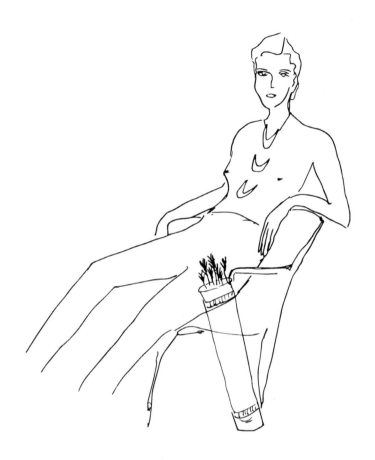

DIANA
THE FREE

In a nutshell, who are you?

I am the goddess of the wilderness. The mountains and the woods are my domain. I'm a hunter and a master archer. My instincts are razor sharp. My aim? Perfect.

I'm not the kind of goddess who enjoys glamorous cocktail parties. I'd rather smell the sap of the pines and feel the crunch of the earth under my feet. My life hinges on the next adventure. I'm most at home in the unknown. I crave experience and above all, freedom.

If you want your brand to encourage adventuring, be fearless, push limits, inspire people to experience their own strength, take them where they've never been before, and help them discover what's out there in this great big world of ours, I'm the goddess for you.

I am Diana—the Free.

What's in your heart?

BRAVERY

If you're going to live life to the fullest, you've got to be brave. I embrace the quest! I tango with the most powerful forces in nature and press ever onward. I always find my way through. At times I do feel afraid, but I never succumb to that fear.

ENTHUSIASM

Why not be wildly enthusiastic? Why not approach life with as much verve as you can muster? If you're going to do something, I say do it with gusto.

INDEPENDENCE

I treasure my independence. I never ask permission or wait for someone else's approval. I go my own way and forge my own path.

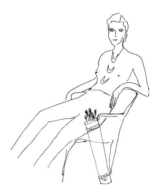

SELF-RELIANCE

In my heart, I know I can handle whatever life throws at me. I follow my instincts, and I trust myself implicitly.

What gifts do you bring?

FREEDOM

I'll encourage your customers to run wild and free. In my presence, they'll feel what it's like to live without limits.

RESILIENCE

I'm a tough but inspiring coach. I'll egg your customers on. I'll help them grow stronger. Around me, they'll feel they can take on anything.

INITIATIVE

I rule new beginnings. I'm great at getting people to press *go*. I'll give your customers the initiative to start something new.

DISCOVERY

I'll lead your customers to surprising places. They'll discover new and amazing things.

What's your style?

MY PERSONALITY

Adventurous. Bold. Brave. Wild.

MY WORDS

Pioneer. Travel. Hunt. Vitality. Aim. Agility. Innovation. Freedom. Beginning. Exploration. Discovery. Onward!

MY SYMBOLS

Mountains. Wilderness. Bow and arrow. Wild beasts. Stag. Deer. Hound. Crescent moon. Wolf. Wind. Amazon. Horse. Jaguar.

MY COLORS

Silver. Green.

Who are your favorite icons?

MAE JEMISON
NASA Astronaut

AMELIA EARHART
Pilot

SERENA WILLIAMS
Tennis Player

ROSIE THE RIVETER
Shipyard and Factory Worker

ZAHA HADID
Architect

WONDER WOMAN
Comic Book Superhero

The most difficult thing is the decision to act, the rest is merely tenacity. The fears are paper tigers. You can do anything you decide to do. You can act to change and control your life; and the procedure, the process is its own reward.

Amelia Earhart

Who is in your constellation?
NIKE, Greek Goddess of Victory

DURGA, "Undefeatable" Hindu goddess

BABA YAGA, Slavic Crone of the Wild Feminine

MARS THE RUGGED, DIANA'S COUNTERPART

MARS: I am the warrior god. I am strong, assertive, and fearless.

Action is what interests me. If something stands in my way, I defy it. I can maneuver over, around, or through any obstacle. I live to test my own limits and the limits of humanity itself.

Rivalry? It only energizes me. I know I can never be vanquished, not even by death.

I am Mars—the Rugged.

MY FAVORITE ICONS

MUHAMMAD ALI
Professional Boxer

LEWIS AND CLARK
North American Explorers

MY WORDS AND SYMBOLS

Unlimited. Primal. Exploration. Speed. Jungle. Sword. Spear. Camouflage. Tiger.

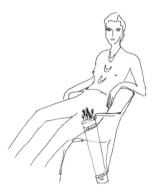

DIANA & MARS
BRANDS

ALWAYS

Since the launch of its breakthrough #RunLikeAGirl campaign, the menstrual products brand has been synonymous with championing girls' confidence; showing how strong and brave girls really are.

NIKE

Closely aligned with Diana, Nike is the winged goddess of victory who inspired not only the name, but the iconic "swoosh" symbol, of the legendary shoe brand.

RAHUA

With its symbol of an Amazonian huntress and ingredients sourced from the rain forest, the haircare brand expresses an energy of wildness and strength.

RIVIAN

The electric vehicle automaker encourages adventuring, showing how its trucks and SUVs are most at home in wild, unspoiled nature.

DIANA BRAND

Caitlin Braam
Founder and CEO of Yonder Cider

Caitlin Braam started Yonder Cider in January 2020 and, as the world shut down, opened a socially distanced hard cider to-go bar out of her home garage. Since that time, she has closed her garage bar and opened the Bale Breaker & Yonder Cider tap room in Seattle.

Yonder has been gaining distribution in retail throughout the Pacific Northwest with three varieties of hard cider, including Dry, Palisades, and Vantage—as well as limited edition seasonals. Yonder's eye-catching cans feature a wolf howling at the moon. Yonder invites drinkers to choose the road less traveled and try this new take on cider, which is far closer to a Negroni than a mug of spiked apple juice. The ethos of the Yonder brand is one of exploration and carving your own path, which reflects Caitlin's own spirit and journey.

Jane McCarthy: What inspired you to start Yonder?

Caitlin Braam: I've been in the food and beverage industry for fifteen years and have worked for many other companies, large and small, helping them build their brands and tell their stories. As I was doing this, I always had my own ideas and felt so passionate about opportunities I saw in the category that people weren't acting on, particularly for cider. I realized the only way I was going to see these ideas realized was for me to do them myself. One day I turned to my husband and said, "I think I want to start my own cidery."

He said, "Finally. We've all been waiting." I said, "Who's we?" He said, "Everyone who knows you."

JM: The heart of Yonder is about inspiring adventure and exploration. At first blush, this isn't the obvious focus for a cider brand. How did you decide to make this the driving passion of your brand?

CB: When you say "cider," most people think of apple trees, of orchards, and a very sweet flavor profile. The preconceived notion that hard cider is sweet, and therefore not for them, has kept a lot of people away from the category. When I was creating the brand, I didn't want to approach it as a traditional cidery might. I wanted to build a kick ass brand that changed perceptions about what the cider experience can be.

In product development, I actually don't think about "cider" at all. I think about cocktails. Our flavors are all based on cocktails. For instance, recently I had this incredible cocktail made with mezcal, pineapple, lime, and cardamom. I went to my product team and said, "I want this flavor to be our new summer seasonal." My team does brilliant things with a direction like that. We do so much blending, and we try combining ingredients in so many different ways. This is what makes us really different and, I think, stand out in the category.

As far as building a brand that is about freedom and a kind of wildness, that's all me. I moved around a lot as a kid (we moved about every two years), and I got very good at adapting to new surroundings. I now have a major travel bug. If you keep me somewhere for more than a couple months, I go stir crazy. So, the Yonder brand is definitely a reflection of who I am. It's also true to who we are as a company. I like to think of our customers enjoying Yonder all over the place and while they're sipping, imagining that somewhere "over yonder" the brand is making and pressing all this beautiful cider that they get to enjoy. One of our slogans is—*Best enjoyed anywhere.*

JM: How did you approach creating the Yonder aesthetic? Your colors (the green and lime, the plum and pink), for instance, are very unique and compelling.

CB: With color, I wanted jewel-tones shared in two-tones. So, something really simple. If you look at the shelf today, it's very busy. A lot of brands have packaging that's got a lot going on, and their packaging varies widely across SKUs. I wanted to do something very consistent across our portfolio, so that it's easy for people to identify every product that comes from Yonder.

Our jewel tones are beautiful, and they stand out. They're high contrast, so you can see them from across a room. Whether you're in a dark bar/restaurant or in a grocery store, you're going to notice Yonder.

No matter what we do within our portfolio and how much we innovate, every product has the tall YONDER running along its side. This way, people can easily identify us and know not only the specific kind of beverage they're buying but also the brand they're supporting. We don't scream "cider" anywhere on our cans. We downplay this piece in favor of the Yonder brand. This is intentional. We're asking people to buy into what Yonder represents and to give us a try vs. getting them to buy into the idea of "cider."

JM: How did you arrive at your brand symbols?

CB: Our wolf and moon reflect our wild and wandering spirit. I think these symbols evoke a feeling in people that's powerful. I mean, the number of people who come up to me and tell me how much they love this tiny little wolf on our can and ask if we can make more merch with the wolf . . . it's kind of amazing.

Wolves, too, they're kind of lone creatures. I've come up in this industry where there aren't many strong women leaders. There just aren't many women-owned companies in the beverage industry. I identify with this idea of being a lone wolf who does her own thing and no matter what she's been told, creates her own path. My attitude is, if you love that, come along for the ride. If you don't, I don't care.

JM: I love that sentiment, and it makes me think of the classic book by Clarissa Pinkola Estés called *Women Who Run With Wolves*. I'm curious, do you have a customer profile or a mindset you focus on?

CB: We reach a pretty wide demographic. We connect with everyone from recent college grads to people in their sixties. A wide range of people identify with Yonder, but I think what ties our customers together is that they all have a willingness to explore and try something new. They're willing to take a chance and go on the adventure of experimenting with this new beverage. You have to be willing to venture outside the box if you're going to try Yonder.

The goal of Yonder, at the end of the day, is to provide a sense of adventure as well as inclusion. We're taking along everyone who wants to go on the ride with us. We're very welcoming. There's no dumb question you can ask about cider. That's a different feeling from other players in the category, and it's part of what makes us unique.

Caitlin Braam
Founder and CEO of Yonder Cider, at her
original cider to-go bar inside her home garage

DIANA AND MARS BRAND

Sophie Bambuck
CMO at The North Face

Since 1966, The North Face has been inspiring people to Never Stop Exploring. Rooted in an ethos of adventure and possibility, the brand has supplied the gear people need and can trust as they venture forth to test and expand their limits. Across decades, The North Face has stayed relevant to each new generation, while continuing to push the boundaries of innovative and sustainable design.

Sophie Bambuck became CMO of The North Face in 2022, following senior roles at Nike, Everlane, and Converse. An energetic, intuitive, and delivery-focused leader, Sophie is an expert at driving brand growth and igniting organizational performance.

Jane McCarthy: I love the statement on The North Face website: *Exploration is our oxygen*. How do you approach weaving that essential ethos into everything you do as a brand?

Sophie Bambuck: Exploration at The North Face is less about doing something that's never been done before, and more about discovering something that's beyond the bounds of what you personally know. We're encouraging you to explore, take risks, and move beyond your comfort zone. I think of exploration as something that's both outward and physical, as well as inward: exploration is a tool for seeking and finding your own true north.

Saying you're about exploration as a brand is one thing, actually living it is another. I try to encourage my team to always seek the new and the different. It's not about doing what we know works today. Internally, we constantly talk about how we're building the future and it's our responsibility as marketers, and as humans, to think about what's next. Otherwise, life gets boring.

JM: The North Face has not only endured for the past fifty-plus years but has managed to remain relevant. How do you think the brand in its current form reflects the initial vision of The North Face founder Doug Tompkins? And then, how has it evolved with culture?

SB: The North Face started as a small shop in Berkeley, California, which sold outdoor equipment. When he founded the company, Doug Tompkins was designing the stuff he and his friends needed to go climbing and stay alive, and he built a business around it—which is smart. There's no better way to start a successful business than to root it in an authentic need paired with a genuine passion for solving that need.

The DNA of The North Face has always been about pushing your limits and trying to see what's next. As long as we stay true to that, we can stand the test of time. Because that's a human trait. It's human nature. And embodying that is going to be relevant to every new generation. Whether conscious or unconscious, everybody has the need to grow and explore.

We've evolved as a brand by pushing beyond the outdoor space into culture and lifestyle. We resonate in these new contexts because our core DNA remains the same. All of our garments are athlete tested and expedition proven. We have a very big team of athletes who are the best in the world at what they do. They want to be on The North Face team not just because we're a cool brand but because our product keeps them alive. There's no better vote of confidence than people trusting you with their life.

So, people can feel confident that if they buy a jacket from The North Face that is warm enough to wear on Everest, it's going to serve them well in a New York City winter. I mean in the middle of January, walking from your apartment to the subway is an expedition, right?

JM: How do you describe The North Face customer? Do you have a customer profile?

SB: We focus on mindsets rather than demographic segments. We've identified four key consumer mindsets for The North Face, which range from "when you want to be performing at your best" to "when you want to look good." The same person can be in several of these mindsets as they go through a single week. For example, a top athlete is going to be in a performance mindset when climbing Half Dome. Later that same week, the same athlete may be attending a film premiere where they shift into the mindset of wanting to look good. The North Face wants to serve that person in both instances.

JM: Why are you personally passionate about being part of The North Face team?

SB: When I left Everlane, I spent some time reflecting on my purpose. I worked with someone to help me do that, and it was fantastic. I landed on three words that describe me: deep thinker, fixer, and explorer. Most people are not deep thinkers and fixers. Usually you're one or the other, so there was an interesting tension there. And then, explorer just made sense.

I love what The North Face stands for. I'm a huge skier and outdoors person. Maybe more than that, though, I think this is a place where I have a chance to make a big impact. I can use my power to help people grow in their lives. And selfishly, I also get to grow in the process. I get to feed my curiosity and feed my need for more adventure, more expansion.

HESTIA
THE SACRED

In a nutshell, who are you?

I am the goddess of the sacred flame. I rule the hearth at the center of every home. I represent the pure spirit of the people.

My essential nature is balance. My very presence purifies. I make clean what has been soiled and make pristine what was once disheveled.

Wherever I go, I bring harmony. I am the great unifier. I hold the lantern high, inspiring faith in dark times. My belief in the goodness of humankind is unshakable.

If you want to calm and soothe people. If you want to be a brand that cleanses and purifies. If you want to invite customers into a space of wellness, peace, and tranquility. If you intend to inspire hope and unity in this world, then I'm an ideal goddess for you.

I am Hestia—the Sacred.

What's in your heart?

PEACE

I care about peace both within my own heart and in the world around me. However rocky outside circumstances may be, I cultivate an inner calm. I beam my inner peacefulness out into the world.

HUMILITY

I bow to all that is sacred and, therefore, I bow to all that is. Being humble and focused on honest service is essential to who I am.

HARMONY

I'm in sync with the rhythm of the world around me. Where others might see division, I feel the essential truth that we are all one. I soak in this feeling of at-oneness with all that is.

PURITY

I act with a purity of heart and of intention. I never have ulterior motives or agendas. Everything I am is in the light.

What gifts do you bring?

HEALING

It's both cleansing and healing to be in my presence. I'll help your customers feel whole and well.

HOPE

Like a jet plane, I lift people above the dark clouds and show them the bright light that is always up there. I give people faith in the future out of the now, just like John Lennon said.

TRANQUILITY

I bring order and simplicity into people's lives. Around me, your customers will feel a greater sense of peace and tranquility.

UNITY

I can help your customers see the commonalities that connect us. I'll remind them of the truth that we are all one.

What's your style?

MY PERSONALITY

Calm. Enlightened. Humble.

MY WORDS

Clean. Meditation. Peace. Unity. Simplicity. Order. Spirit. Faith. Holistic. Pure. Ceremony. Haven. Essence. Healing. Wellness. Equanimity.

MY SYMBOLS

Light. Candle. Lantern. Flame. Hearth. Lotus. Snow. Swan. Camellia. Grove. Dove. Altar. Wings. Feathers. Circle. Desert. Lark. Grove. Herbs. Amethyst. Incense. Smoke.

MY COLORS

White. Blue. Violet.

Who are your favorite icons?

PEACE PILGRIM

Peace Activist

MARIE KONDO

Tidying-Up Expert

RUPI KAUR

Poet

YOKO ONO

Artist

ANNA HALPRIN

Dancer

MARIANNE WILLIAMSON

Spiritual Teacher

ENYA

Singer/Songwriter

G ive peace a chance and let's hope that one day we will all live in peace.

Yoko Ono

Who is in your constellation?

WHITE BUFFALO WOMAN, Lakota Spirit of Peace

BRIGID, Celtic Goddess of Light and Healing

HYGIEIA, Greek Goddess of Health

BEREHYNIA, Slavic Goddess of the Hearth

APOLLO THE SHINING, HESTIA'S COUNTERPART

APOLLO: I am the god of virtue. I urge moderation in all things. As the patron of healing, I support good habits that contribute to overall wellness.

When I strum my lyre, I vibrate the cosmos. At one with the universe, I flow with the currents. I move to the music of the spheres, riding my chariot close to the sun.

I am Apollo—the Shining.

MY FAVORITE ICONS

PARAHAMANSA YOGANANDA
Hindu Monk, Yogi, and Guru

ECKHART TOLLE
Spiritual Teacher

MY WORDS AND SYMBOLS

Health. Moderation. Medicine. Providence. Prophecy. Goodness. Sun. Lyre. Chariot. Caduceus. Condor.

HESTIA & APOLLO
BRANDS

GOOP

The GOOP brand is synonymous with the high standards of its founder Gwyneth Paltrow. GOOP is famous for embracing an array of approaches to wellness and healing.

RITUAL

The supplements brand offers people a pure vitamin, without the junk. With Ritual, taking your daily vitamin is a small, yet vital ceremony.

MUJI

The Japanese household goods brand is known for its minimal design aesthetic. Muji believes that simplicity is at the heart of universality.

DR. BRONNER'S

The all-natural soap and hygiene brand emphasizes humanity's essential oneness, built upon Emanuel Bronner's peace plan for uniting all those traveling on this spaceship we call Earth.

HESTIA BRAND

Susan Griffin-Black
Co-Founder and Co-CEO of EO Products

A pioneer in the wellness space, Susan Griffin-Black co-founded EO Products with Brad Black in 1995. Since that time, the wellness industry has seen massive growth and EO has grown with it. EO offers an array of natural, essential oil-infused bath and body products from shower gel to hand wipes to deodorant spray. As the brand has expanded, its mission has remained the same—To honor the well-being of all people and the planet we share.

EO plays a vital role in people's self-care rituals in a way that is simple, clean, and calming. The brand is exacting and transparent about each ingredient that goes into every bottle. As a B Corp, EO is committed not only to providing trusted, high quality products but also to making them with integrity in their family-owned, zero-waste factory in San Rafael, CA.

While Co-CEO of EO Products for the past twenty-eight-plus years, Susan Griffin-Black has also been a devoted student of Zen Buddhism. Susan continuously endeavors to integrate her own values and spiritual practice with the values and practices of EO Products.

Jane McCarthy: You founded EO Products in 1995. Why did you feel this company needed to exist in the world at that time and why were you passionate about bringing these particular products to market?

Susan Griffin-Black: Prior to EO, I was a clothing designer for Esprit, working for the late Doug Tompkins. So, I was already a product person. I was always intrigued by the cultural aspects of products. I liked asking, "Why this? Why now? What does this mean to me? What does this mean to you?"

I'd promised myself Esprit was my last gig. The only reason I was doing it was because Doug was very interested in the environment and the way we make things. He had a strong belief that we could make things in a kinder, gentler way. That job was a portal to learning about all sorts of things I was interested in. When Doug sold the company to his partner, I started thinking about what to do next. I was on a shopping trip in London, and I found myself at Neal's Yard in Covent Garden. Directly in front of me was this incredible apothecary. I walked in, and it smelled so fresh and natural. It was amazing and completely different from how Bloomingdale's or those popular nineties stores like Pier 1 Imports smelled at the time, which was very chemical and toxic. I picked up this little bottle of lavender oil and I thought, *This is what I want to do.*

Above the apothecary, there was an acupuncturist and a homeopath. You could see a healer who would suggest a remedy, and then go downstairs to have your prescription filled. The apothecary made tinctures and remedies of all kinds. They also had bath and body care products and books . . . It was wonderful. When I got back to the States, I decided to start studying aromatherapy and herbal medicine. I also took a crash course in cosmetic chemistry.

I think the reason EO needed to exist was that the chemical era, which we thought was bringing all sorts of goodness along with convenience, was actually not so beneficial. Essential oils seemed like an antidote to what was going on at the time. I wanted to give people a moment of realness that connected them to the present moment and engaged their senses with natural elements instead of toxic, cheap ingredients.

You know, there's an obvious, palpable difference between a fake rose and a real one. From ten feet away, you may not be able to tell them apart, but as you get up close, the vitality, the fragrance, the biological and physiological connection with the real rose cannot be replicated.

Kate McAndrew: What was your initial marketing strategy?

SGB: When we started, our focus was on getting distribution at natural food stores. We wanted to be in places where food was seen as medicine. In 1997, we started selling at Whole Foods. At that time, I think there were maybe only forty stores, and we had to sell-in to each individual store. Whole Foods, of course, went regional and ultimately, global.

Growing up within the natural products industry was so refreshing compared to my previous experience in apparel. Since we never raised money from institutional investors, we were able to grow the way we wanted to. Margin was not our first priority. Our priority was to offer the highest quality product at a reasonable price, get our products out there, and earn a living doing it. We took our lead from companies like Patagonia and Ben & Jerry's. We were really a Benefit-corporation before that was a thing. Of course, if there's no margin, there's no mission. We were aware of that, but we didn't want to sell EO products at a luxury price point.

JM: Your packaging is beautifully simple and your signature blue color is, at this point, iconic. How did you arrive at the aesthetic for your brand?

SGB: I wanted the brand to be clean and modern so I chose a typography that was very similar to *Vogue*. And then, we adopted the blue color of the bottles that were sold at Neal's Yard. That blue has remained our go-to color. When people don't know what EO is, or what it stands for, they still know the blue bottles. That's how they recognize us. The bottles really are beautiful. Blue is such a universally calming color.

JM: How did you decide to focus on playing a role in people's self-care rituals and giving people this feeling of tranquility and calm?

SGB: I started meditating in the bathtub when my son was about one-and-a-half (he's now thirty-seven), because that was the only place where I felt it was reasonable to ask for a bit of space. He'd wander in and out of the bathroom, and sometimes he'd sit quietly in there with me. That was really the origin of my meditation practice. I've now been a student of Zen Buddhism for the past thirty-plus years. The ritual of taking a pause, the sacred pause, to check in and see if we're actually here and if we have the capacity to be available to the moment, is about nurturing our inner life. It's a way of being that then gets reflected outward. I think applying essential oils, taking care of our bodies, can be part of that sacred pause.

KM: The wellness space has gone through extraordinary changes since you started EO. Do you have any advice for founders on how to not just grow, but also, endure?

SGB: I think you have to be in it in a way that is aligned with your own values and purpose in life. Being in business is challenging. Over the years, I can give you so many examples of times where we veered off course and had to get back to that central why we're doing what we're doing. Growth can be seductive. You have to keep going back to your core values to be sure you're in alignment. Otherwise, it's so easy to drift. I've found that to be a constant struggle.

We've been in business for twenty-eight years, and the reason we've stayed in business is our customers, who keep coming back and buying the products. They're the ones who evaluate us.

HESTIA BRAND

Laura Modi
Co-Founder and CEO of Bobbie

After Laura Modi gave birth to her first child, she struggled with feeding. Turning to formula, she was met with both a wave of guilt and a shock at the ingredients that were in the baby formulas then available on the shelf. Laura was determined to bring a simple, organic baby formula to market.

Laura and her "work-wife" from their days at Airbnb, Sarah Hardy, founded Bobbie in 2018. In their first year, Bobbie multiplied their revenue projections by more than five times. And in year two, Bobbie broke $100 million as a profitable business. This company is personal for me (Kate!) as I had the distinct honor of being Bobbie's first investor and still sit on the Bobbie board.

As a brand, Bobbie focuses on bringing parents peace of mind. As Bobbie puts it, *Parenting is complicated. Our baby formula is simple.*

Kate McAndrew: Can you speak to your journey in delivering a product that parents can truly trust? I remember your initial statement on the Bobbie website was—*We lost sleep over this so you don't have to.*

Laura Modi: You know, I didn't randomly decide to start a formula company. When my daughter at four days old wasn't latching to my breast, I started to experience guilt, and I knew there had to be a better way. At night, I racked my brain and researched everything I could about the marketplace. I got a mini PhD in formula. For two years, I poured my heart into this and made spreadsheets and considered if I could really do it, if I could afford to leave my job at Airbnb and invest in the business. I really wanted to make this my life's work. It was a huge leap. I fully committed to doing this when I was pregnant with my second kid, and I remember thinking, *I will not have this kid until there's a better formula on the market.*

It took a bit longer, but every single ounce of me believed I could do it better. I decided, I will lose sleep over this until there is a better product on the market, and I will ensure every parent experiences the trust and peace of mind that I didn't get to have.

In the early days, as we were pitching the members of the medical community, we found they felt this passion too. The gatekeepers who were involved in our getting FDA approval wanted to be sure this wasn't just a money-making machine and they came to the conviction that we were doing our absolute every-thing for this business. We didn't miss the mark on anything.

KM: At the time Bobbie launched, what did other formula brands look like?

LM: The brands in the category at that time felt like Boomer brands. They hadn't evolved in decades. Most were positioned as a medical solution for a woman fail-ing to feed her baby. Nothing about these brands seemed to be having a conver-sation with a real customer. They felt like pharma brands.

KM: Right, Bobbie felt so fresh in the category with your super clean can. How did you arrive at your signature Irish green and the amazing line drawing of the cow that's still on your packaging today?

LM: Bobbie's first employee was Aoife A., my Irish gal pal for life. She and I were working with a branding firm in New York and something wasn't landing. We were flying back from New York and we were feeling meh about the design work we'd seen. We were like, it's good, but, meh. And we were so in it, living and breathing Bobbie. We just knew we could do better with the brand. Aoife decid-ed to do a search on Google, and she found this line drawing of a cow. She turned to me on the airplane and she said, "What do you think of this?" I was like, "It's stunning. It's perfect." And it really was. I love that it's a singular line drawing. I'm obsessed with singular line drawings because to me they're an expression of the journey that keeps going, that has no end. So, we bought the cow on the plane and that was it.

    We chose green as our brand color, because it expresses grass-fed, clean, and organic. Our shade of Kelly Green is gorgeous. I don't think I thought twice about it. It was just so obvious. And then our Boobs to Bottle logo is another single line drawing.

KM: I love that logo. I wear my Boobs to Bottle shirt all the time. I love how my son (one of the first to be fed with Bobbie's formula) points at it and says, "Boobs! Bottle!" What's so great about that logo is it communicates that it's not either breast milk OR formula. The reality is many women are feeding their babies with a mix of both.

LM: I randomly drew the concept for the Boobs to Bottle logo on the back of a bank envelope that was sitting on my desk. I sent the picture over to my sister-in-law, and she turned it into a vector drawing . . . The more you grow, the more money you get, it's easy to think you need to add ten people to your team and spend a million dollars on design. But we talk all the time about how everything that is core to who we are was honestly done on the back of an envelope.

KM: How have customers and particularly, influencers, helped you tell your story?

LM: Bobbie's mission goes far beyond selling formula, which impacts our approach with influencers. We encourage them to use their platforms to change the conversation and help remove the stigma around formula feeding. It's less about selling the product and more about using their platforms for good. Celebrity influencers have done things like feed babies during the formula shortage, sponsor double mastectomy moms, and support solutions for the Black maternal mortality crisis.

   When celebrities post about Bobbie, we don't guide what they say about us. We want them to share what's in their heart. Laura Dern was one of the first celebrities to post about Bobbie. She shared a reflection from when she was a young mother and had to turn to formula for her baby. There's nothing fake about these posts.

KM: Can you talk a little bit about how Bobbie handled the formula shortage in 2022 and the decisions you made during that crisis?

LM: We came to a hard crossroads, which I'll never forget. Our Head of Growth was sitting with me and she said, "Laura, we have a dilemma. We are going through product faster than we can replenish it." Keep in mind, this woman's job is to put her foot on the pedal and drive our business forward. And she said, "I've never seen this sort of growth rate, but I'm not sure when we're going to get more product. We have two days before we will have grown past our ability to have enough product to serve this growth rate." She told me that if we wanted to guarantee we'd have enough product to serve our existing subscribers through the end of their feeding journeys, we needed to turn our site off.

   Sitting here now it seems obvious that the right decision was to turn off the site, but it wasn't obvious then. We had to make the call, and I'm proud we made the decision we did. I think we were able to make that choice because we kept thinking about what it would be like to be one of these parents up late at night worrying about our baby. We couldn't have a parent saying, "Shit, Bobbie promised me this product and now how am I going to find food?" We couldn't let that happen, so we prioritized peace of mind over profit and turned off the site for seven months.

KM: Bobbie was unique because it was the first direct-to-consumer infant formula with a subscription offering. You knew who your customers were and you could predict how much formula they would need to feed their baby. And from there, you were bringing people onto a waitlist and only committing to customers you knew you could provide for, for their whole feeding journeys. When they committed to you, you committed to them. That was incredibly difficult to do operationally, but I think it was profound in the sense that you truly walked the walk in terms of delivering peace of mind to your customers.

LM: It was a big financial question because, keep in mind, we were sitting on millions and millions of dollars of inventory. We were locking up our cash position but our customers' loyalty carried us through.

Laura Modi
Co-Founder and CEO of Bobbie

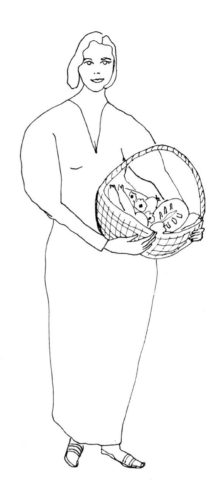

DEMETER
THE LOVE

In a nutshell, who are you?

I am the mother goddess. I'm a mother not only to children but to animals, plants, and the whole natural world.

I'm a most compassionate goddess. I feel the suffering of others acutely and always do my utmost to make things better for those in need, offering comfort wherever I can.

I'm the goddess of the harvest. I represent the bounty of Earth. I am the abundant supply! And what is my abundant warmth and tenderness born from? Love, of course.

If you want to be a caring and compassionate brand. If you want to nourish and nurture. If you want to offer protection and scoop your customers up in a giant embrace, knock on my door.

I am Demeter—the Love.

What's in your heart?

COMPASSION

My heart is filled with compassion. I feel for others and care deeply about their well-being.

INCLUSIVITY

I value inclusivity. I want to wrap my arms around the whole world!

GENEROSITY

I'm generous not only in terms of material wealth but also in my praise and appreciation of others. I spread my love far and wide.

PROTECTION

I believe that everyone deserves to feel safe and protected in this world. I feel it's my responsibility to shelter the vulnerable. If threatened, I can be ferocious as a mother bear protecting her cub.

What gifts do you bring?

SAFETY

I'll help your customers feel secure and well taken care of.

ACCEPTANCE

I'll love your customers for exactly who they are, accepting them without question or critique. In my presence, they won't be judged. They'll feel loved.

PLENTY

I'll remind your customers of Earth's great bounty. Around me, they'll feel the abundant energy of regenerative nature.

NOURISHMENT

I'll nourish your customers and help them feel a wholesome satisfaction. The true sustenance.

What's your style?

MY PERSONALITY

Warm. Accepting. Supportive. Compassionate.

MY WORDS

Care. Bounty. Understanding. Embrace. Tenderness. Mother. Family. Sustenance. Nourishment. Shelter. Regeneration. Protection.

MY SYMBOLS

Cornucopia. Harvest. Farm. Full Moon. Milk. Fields. Grain. Bread. Corn. Pumpkin. Cow. Autumn. Womb. Bear. Heart. Soup. Basket. Mud. Valley. Seeds. Hen. Egg.

MY COLORS

Orange. Amber. Green. Jade.

Who are your favorite icons?

JANE GOODALL
Primatologist and Conservation Activist

ALICE WATERS
Founder of Chez Panisse

AMMA
Hindu Spiritual Leader—"The Hugging Saint"

OPRAH
Media Giant and Philanthropist

CATELYN STARK
Game of Thrones Matriarch

CANDY LIGHTNER
Founder of Mothers Against Drunk Driving

MARMEE
Little Women Matriarch

L eadership is about empathy.
Oprah Winfrey

Who is in your constellation?
GUANYIN, Bodhisattva of Compassion

AMBIKA, Hindu Mother Goddess

ASASE YAA, Akan Goddess of Earth and Fertility

MOTHER MARY, Christian Virgin Mother

GAIA, Greek Earth Mother

MAMA COCHA, Incan Sea Mother

POSEIDON THE DEEP, DEMETER'S COUNTERPART

POSEIDON: I am the god of the sea. I'm known for the intensity of my emotion. My rage is a tempest. A perfect storm. Yet, I can also be mellow. A placid sea that mirrors the heavens. Whatever I feel, I feel it deeply.

I enjoy philosophy and I write poetry. I can be quite nostalgic. Some even call me sentimental. I spend my days looking out upon the vast expanse of ocean, contemplating the nature of memory, of time, of our very existence.

I am Poseidon—the Deep.

MY FAVORITE ICONS

CARL JUNG
Psychiatrist and Psychoanalyst

WALT WHITMAN
American Poet and Essayist

MY WORDS AND SYMBOLS

Poetry. Philosophy. Nostalgia. Sublime. Ocean. Waves. Trident. Troubadour. Twilight.

SUBARU

Subaru emphasizes the safety of its cars in service of protecting the people you love most. Love is at the heart of everything the brand does.

MADRE MEZCAL

The artisanal spirits brand honors Mother Earth while exuding a rooted, folk art sensibility.

PLENTY

The indoor vertical farm brand delivers fresh, flavorful, pesticide-free greens to your grocery aisle in a way that uses less water and land. Nurturing nature is at the heart of the Plenty brand.

MASTERCARD

With its long-running Priceless campaign, the credit card brand evokes moments of shared connection that touch on the deep meaning of life.

DEMETER BRAND

Cristiana Sadigianis
Founder of Oracle Oil

In 2019, Cristiana Sadigianis launched the premium, small-batch Greek olive oil, Oracle Oil. Made from 100% organic Koroneiki olives, the olive oil is sourced from a collective of sustainable farms in Laconia, Greece—including one belonging to Cristiana's own family, where they have been making olive oil for generations.

On the shelf, Oracle Oil is a vision to behold with its unmistakable, Aegean blue bottle and unique watercolor imagery. The brand evokes the ancient feminine, the spirit of fertility and of abundance.

Jane McCarthy: What inspired you to start Oracle Oil?

Cristiana Sadigianis: My parents were born in Greece and growing up, I spent all my summers there. Both sides of my family were agrarians and had farms. In the summer, I lived with my grandparents. The life there was simple and very much revolved around food. This idea of nourishment as an expression of love runs deep in Greek culture. There was sort of this transmission of love through food that I experienced with my grandmother and mother. We always spent a lot of time discussing meals. In a day, we'd take a trip to the butcher, and another to the fishmonger, and so on. I'd take a long walk, pick some figs, swim in the sea, and go back and help prepare the food.

As I approached my late thirties, I began to feel very nostalgic for those summers in Greece. I was living in New York working as a photo producer in both the commercial and fine art space, but my heart was pulling me toward those summers. I felt haunted by these memories of my uncle herding sheep and a yearning for the land itself, like I was being called back to it.

My production work, although adventurous and exciting at times, was draining and emotionally depleting, and so I'd become interested in food as nourishment, rather than sustenance. Over the years, I'd managed to take courses with the Natural Gourmet Institute, and I'd received a certificate from the Institute for Integrative Nutrition, but things didn't really click into place until I took an olive oil sommelier class. There are these classes where you taste like a hundred different olive oils, and olive oil nerds come to New York from all over Europe to teach you about the nuances of the oils. That class set me on my path. We have olive groves on both sides of the family, and up until that point, had only produced enough for ourselves and our community, but I knew I could figure out a way to produce and sell it.

JM: What was that process like?

CS: Our family only had about two thousand trees, so I knew I'd need more olives. I set off on an exploratory trip in 2018 and began to source from neighboring organic farms who had the same variety of olives. It's been amazing to be able to support these farmers who weren't making very much money before and to pay them well.

It has been challenging to work in Greece as a female founder. The country is sadly still steeped in old patriarchal ways, and the olive oil industry is largely dominated by men. Beyond that, though, it has been a homecoming, a return to the land.

Kate McAndrew: It's powerful that you chose to source your oil from the olive groves that belong to your family instead of finding a generic olive oil producer and building a brand around a mass product. It's a very particular choice to make. In many ways, you are sacrificing operational simplicity in order to truly bring forth the familial harvest.

CS: It is harder. The farm is so small, and we are meticulous about harvesting early, which yields a much lower supply. However, the quality is phenomenal. If you wait to harvest the olives later in the season, they are plumper, juicier, and produce more oil, but the antioxidant and polyphenol yield is much lower. So, we choose to harvest the olives when they are still green and a little bit unripe.

We also don't prune the trees very much. We let them grow wilder than a lot of farms, and we don't use any pesticides or cheap fertilizers. This involves more time and greater cost, but we'd never compromise on that. The priority has been on quality vs. profit. In some ways I've made things harder for myself, but I was never going to do it any other way.

JM: How did you approach building your brand?

CS: My journey of building the narrative and the packaging—how the olive oil was going to be transmitted to the world—was very much a bootstrapping experience. I never hired a branding agency. I really worked on it from an intuitive place and went with what felt right.

JM: You use blue watercolor paint both in your logo and on your label. In a world full of graphic design, that's quite an unusual choice and it's part of what makes your bottle beam brightly on the shelf. It looks so elevated and inviting. How did you arrive at this aesthetic?

CS: The blue represents the sea to me, which has played a huge role in my life. Since I was young, I have felt so connected to it. The use of watercolor made sense to me as a representation of the ocean, because it's fluid, not stagnant or finite. At the time I was working on developing the identity for the brand, I went to the Modigliani exhibition at the Jewish Museum. I was very inspired by Modigliani's drawing of the Caryatids.

The Caryatids are sculpted female figures that serve as architectural support in the place of a column or a pillar—they gracefully hold the weight of sacred temples with their heads alone. The Caryatid, Cycladic sculpture, and the Oracle of Delphi (where my mother was born) felt like the perfect symbol of fertility and regeneration. These sculptures of the female form with very round bellies, holding the vessel or the amphora, felt deeply feminine to me and an expression of the feminine as a source of containment and holding.

I knew I wanted to work with an artist to develop the logo and label. I have a good friend named Alejandro Cardenas who is a painter. I was lucky he was interested and available to help me flesh out my vision. I sent Alejandro a bunch of images of Caryatids and imagery of the land in Greece, particularly of the trees and the Cycladic Islands, and he got started . . .

Everything about the process of creating the packaging was deeply personal. I think the bottle in the end is an expression of my connection to the ancestral feminine, through my mother and grandmother, and to the larger feminine—mother earth.

JM: I'm curious, what inspired you to expand your product line to include body oil? It's not common for a brand to move beyond the food category into beauty.

CS: A lot of customers were writing to tell us they were using our olive oil on their bodies. One customer in particular wrote to tell us that she had used the oil on her face and her acne had completely cleared up. I was like, wow, I never had that intention for the oil. I began thinking back to how my grandmother would anoint herself with the olive oil. She would put it on her body and her face, morning and night. When I was a teenager, I was using Noxzema and Clearasil, and I remember thinking—can you trust old people? I had this assumption that what my grandmother was using as a skin remedy was outdated. It's nice to have come around to see the benefits of high-quality olive oil for your skin.

When I started looking at the beauty category, I noticed brands were using a lot of seed oils. There wasn't much olive oil available in skin products. I began working with a chemist and a botanist to develop a really nice blend. We ventured off the beaten path to find these endemic, wild herbs and concocted a formula for the body oil that includes ingredients from the mountain and the sea. We sourced this amazing sea fennel that grows on rocks along the water. I think with its ingredients, and its scent, the body oil is transporting. It feels like a breezy day on the Aegean.

Cristiana Sadigianis
Founder of Oracle Oil

DEMETER & POSEIDON BRAND

Julia Marsh
Co-Founder of Sway

Sway is an early stage startup based in Oakland, CA, that harnesses the power of seaweed to create replacements for plastic packaging. The company was founded by Julia Marsh, Leland Maschmeyer, and Matt Mayes in 2020. Seaweed is the foundation of all Sway products, which mimic the compelling qualities of plastic without the downsides. Utilizing the natural polymers contained in seaweed, they are able to optimize and scale the solutions nature has already given.

Sway's products serve a wide range of applications and industries, including packaging for apparel, home goods, cosmetics, and food. Unlike many business-to-business (B2B) companies whose branding is highly functional and technical, the Sway brand is warm and approachable. With open arms, Sway communications invite people to experience the abundance of the sea.

In 2023, Sway won the Tom Ford Plastic Innovation Prize. They have raised $2.5 million in venture capital to fund their mission.

Kate McAndrew: How did you decide to start Sway?

Julia Marsh: I started out working as a designer for startups and was typically the person helping to source materials. At that time, I was led by the idea that design was for beauty. But I was fundamentally feeding the plastic problem through my designs. I started pitching decision-makers on using alternative materials, but frequently got turned down (for many different reasons).

I went for my Master's at the School of Visual Arts in New York, and it was there that I became obsessed with the circular economy, and particularly its third pillar, which is to replenish natural systems. That led me down the rabbit hole of regenerative design.

KM: How did you come up with the idea of using seaweed for packaging?

JM: Initially, my focus was simply on flexible plastic packaging–bags, wrappers, pouches. These are ubiquitous materials that most people don't think about, and they make up an enormous portion of the environmental pollution on this planet. Plastic is petroleum, and the petroleum industry is betting on flexible plastics to save itself.

I started thinking about replacing plastic, which is one of the fundamental building blocks of modern society, in a way that actually replenishes systems. A positive climate future is one where people aren't necessarily inconvenienced–instead, we create access to familiar systems that bake in value along the way, actually giving life in the process. To do that, you need an amazing feedstock and an amazing supply chain.

I was raised in the Monterey Bay area in California (my family actually worked for the Monterey Bay Aquarium!), so I come from a culture of caring about the environment–and especially the ocean. I learned that seaweed contains natural polymers. I also learned that from an economic standpoint, it is a super productive crop. Seaweed grows thirty times faster than corn or sugarcane, and doesn't require inputs like fresh water, or land, or pesticides. This is the dream scenario for a feedstock of the future! I never looked back.

KM: On Sway's website, you have a repeated scroll of the tagline *The Future is Regenerative.* Can you paint a picture for us of what that regenerative future looks like?

JM: With each of the new materials we are designing, our goal is to replenish natural and social systems at every step of the supply chain. Our plan is not to build another extractive system, but instead, one that actually gives more than it takes.

At first, that happens through our sourcing strategy. Beyond the productivity and low-intensity of seaweed cultivation, there are all these value-adds. Seaweed farms sequester carbon and offer resilient employment to coastal communities.

After it's harvested, seaweed can bring its regenerative qualities to the plastic industry. We've designed Sway technology to be fully compatible with traditional infrastructure, and I love the fact that we get to approach plastic manufacturers and say, "We've designed a totally new material, and you can enable positive change just by producing it with us. It performs, it's more efficient, and it's less wasteful!"

And then, finally, you have the consumer. We're really a business-to-business-to-consumer company (B2B2C). Companies pay us, but ultimately, our product ends up in the hands of the consumer. The consumer has an opportunity to feel that they are also contributing when they purchase products packaged by Sway and compost the packaging after use. Our materials decompose naturally and have nutrient content that actually adds value to the soil. We want to close the loop of biological circularity.

In a regenerative future, home and industrial composting will be the norm. That's certainly the biggest piece of the puzzle where we need investment in infrastructure and public policy to help enable that future.

KM: Who are your beachhead customers? Can you share some examples of brands you're working with?

JM: At the moment, we're focused on partnering with brands in the fashion and home goods categories where the requirements for packaging are easier to meet. In fashion, the biggest need is for dust guards that protect the garments. About 180 billion plastic polybags are used every single year in the fashion industry alone, so there's a huge need for better alternatives. We recently won first place in the Tom Ford Plastic Innovation Prize, which is focused on this issue of polybags in the fashion industry. Through that prize, we were matched with a range of different fashion brands, including J. Crew, which has an amazing team. They care so deeply about actually solving this problem and helping a company like Sway scale.

    We also work with smaller, domestic brands where we can immediately service their packaging needs. Our first ever public-facing pilots were with Graf Lantz, a woolen goods company based in Los Angeles. And we worked with Ales Grey, a bio-based footwear company (also based in LA). Both of those brands have been enthusiastic about sharing the Sway story and helping us gather customer feedback, which can then guide how we work with larger scale partners and launches.

KM: Sway's voice is very accessible, and it's warm. On your site, you talk about the inherent generosity of the ocean and the benevolent qualities of seaweed—it's emotional and abundant language. How did you decide to communicate in this way?

JM: It's a priority to us that Sway feels as inviting as possible. Without accessibility, we can't make a real impact. A lot of climate solutions are presented in a scientific, technical way that is alienating to people. I'm a non-technical founder running a material science company, and I often get tripped up on certain scientific terminology and will ask my polymer scientists to help me understand. Typically, the answer is actually very simple. So much of innovation is not as complex as we think it is. I wanted our brand voice to reflect this and be welcoming to all people regardless of their background.

MAIDEN
PERSEPHONE
THE DREAM

In a nutshell, who are you?

I am the maiden goddess. Cloaked in my innocence, my youth is a perpetual spring. I spend my days chatting with fairies, frolicking through the halls of Olympus, and picking wildflowers in fragrant meadows. Everything I do has a touch of sweetness and delight.

My imagination knows no bounds. I can go far out. For me, fantasy and reality blend into one perfect dream.

I have the aura of a mystic. I can see beyond the surface of things into the wonder and magic of many dimensions. I sense the possibility all around us. I believe in what can be even if it has not yet manifested on the material plane.

If you want to invite your customers into a world of wonder. If you want your brand to be youthful and sweet. If you intend to inspire blue sky imagining and tap into the child living within all of us, I'm your goddess.

I am Maiden Persephone—the Dream.

What's in your heart?

SWEETNESS

I appreciate sweetness in life, which is why I sprinkle a bit of fairy dust on everything I touch.

WONDER

I never lost my child-like eyes. I see just how magical and marvelous the world actually is.

OPENNESS

I move through the world with "a beginner's mindset" coming to life with a genuine openness.

IMAGINATION

Nothing brings me more pleasure than dreaming up new ideas for the miraculous things that might one day be real. Give me a sketchpad, and I'll draw you a whole universe you might just want to step into.

What gifts do you bring?

DELIGHT

I surprise, mesmerize, and hypnotize. I offer moments of sheer delight. By piling on the fantastical, the unusual, and the surreal, I'll bring your customers all manner of ecstatic amusement.

LIGHTNESS

Around me, people feel carefree. Your customers will experience a lightness of being as they're transported out of their everyday and into an otherworldly moment that feels fresh and inspiring.

RE-ENCHANTMENT

I'll help your customers become reacquainted with the children they once were. They'll re-experience the wonder and magic in things.

POSSIBILITY

I'll open the door for your customers to dream bright and beautiful dreams. In my presence, they'll feel a sense of vibrant possibility.

What's your style?

MY PERSONALITY

Carefree. Whimsical. Innocent. Mystic.

MY WORDS

Enchantment. Fantasy. Youth. Ideal. Sweetness. Darling. Imagine. Magic. Possibility. Surreal. Frolic. Delight. Charm.

MY SYMBOLS

Wildflower. Daisy. Strawberry. Blueberry. Fairy. Unicorn. Rainbow. Butterfly. Ribbons. Clouds. Meadow. Bluebird. Opal. Peach. Cherry. Linen. Dew. Plum. Violet. Bubbles. Poppy. Spring. Waterfall. Stars.

MY COLORS

Pastels. Rainbow.

Who are your favorite icons?

BJÖRK
Singer-Songwriter

BETSEY JOHNSON
Fashion Designer

SOPHIA COPPOLA
Director

MARY BLAIR
Artist and Animator

KATE BUSH
Singer-Songwriter

MARY POPPINS
Nanny

ISABEL ALLENDE
Writer

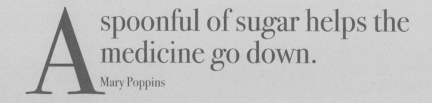

A spoonful of sugar helps the medicine go down.
Mary Poppins

Who is in your constellation?

FIRTOS, Queen of the Good Hungarian Fairies

HINE-PIKOHU-RANGI, Māori Mist Maiden

FLORA, Roman Goddess of Flowers

PAN THE MISCHIEF, MAIDEN PERSEPHONE'S COUNTERPART

PAN: I am the trickster god. Yes, I'm a mischief maker. A real wile coyote.

Though many write me off as a fool, I have a way of noticing things most "practical" people do not. I'm in on the cosmic joke. I illuminate the weird and wonderful absurdities of life. I bring humor to any situation. For me, nothing is serious. Life is a carnival of the silly, the odd, and the fanciful.

I'm never dull, and I love a spectacle! I'm known for throwing epic parties in the woods where I bang on my drum and dance a jiggy jig jig.

I am Pan—the Mischief.

MY FAVORITE ICONS

HARRY STYLES
Musician and Actor

JIM CARREY
Actor and Comedian

MY WORDS AND SYMBOLS

Jokes. Comic. Eccentric. Absurd. Idiot Savant. Odd. Prankster. Parade. Flute. Elves. Coyote. Grapes. Wine. Monkey.

MAIDEN PERSEPHONE & PAN BRANDS

KIN EUPHORICS

The functional beverage brand has a mystic mindset, opening portals to new dimensions of experience.

MEGABABE

The innovative body brand is out to end thigh-chafing and under arm odor in the cutest, brightest way possible.

RODARTE

The fashion brand is known for its dreamy world-building and whimsical incorporation of bows, florals, and tulle.

VACATION

The sunscreen brand is a trip back to 1980s Miami complete with that sunscreen scent you remember oh-so-well, Eighties-style print ads, and product in whipped cream cans that are hilarious and fun.

MAIDEN PERSEPHONE BRAND

Sashee Chandran
Founder and CEO of Tea Drops

In 2015, Sashee Chandran launched Tea Drops, an innovative tea company that creates organic, bagless tea experiences. The brand's colorful, whimsical aesthetic mixed with its entirely unique form factor culminates in a tea moment that is transporting.

Tea Drops can be found in over two thousand retail stores nationwide, as well as online. In 2021, *Inc. Magazine* named Sashee Chandran one of its Top 100 Female Founders.

Jane McCarthy: What inspired you to start Tea Drops?

Sashee Chandran: I come from a pretty tea-rich household. Both of my parents are immigrants who came to the United States from countries that are steeped in tea culture (my mom is Chinese and my dad is from Sri Lanka). Whenever I was sick, my mom would make me chrysanthemum Chinese tea and when I went to my paternal grandmother's house, she would make me a version of chai tea. So, I've always associated tea with these very defining and important childhood memories. Then when I was a teenager, my friends and I would go to Starbucks, get a chai tea together, and talk. To me it was this special beverage that sparked connection and a feeling of openness.

   After college, I started working in an office and would make loose leaf tea at my desk. I found that process to be very cumbersome and inconvenient when working in a fast-paced environment, which sent me on a quest to explore the format of tea. We've been preparing tea in the same way for thousands of years. The only true innovation has been with the tea bag, which was introduced in the early 1900s. In my research, I learned that most tea bags are either bleached or filled with microplastics. They're also usually made with tea dust, which is less flavorful than loose leaf tea. And so, my intention became to find a new format that provided the quality and purity of loose leaf tea while offering the convenience of a tea bag.

JM: How did you ultimately land on the Tea Drops format?

SC: I was at the mall one day, and I walked into a Lush store. At that time, they were known for their bath bombs. If you've ever taken a bath with a bath bomb, then you know how the colors and scents meld together to create this magical experience. I was really inspired by that format and thought I could make something like it for tea. So, I spent the next year and a half making prototypes, which led me to our chai tea drop.

JM: As you've built the world of your brand around this innovative format, what kind of experience do you aim to give your customers?

SC: We use a lot of color to connote different feelings and to bring a whimsical aspect to tea drinking. It's kind of a dreamy experience that takes you out of your normal, everyday world and grounds you to something else, whether that's a deeper connection with yourself or with someone you're sharing the tea with.

JM: You developed a limited edition collection with Hello Kitty. How did that partnership come about?

SC: Hello Kitty actually approached us and said that they liked our branding and our values and wanted to do something together. I was born in the eighties and grew up with Hello Kitty and Sanrio. I thought a lot of our customers probably had a similar, kind of nostalgic connection to Hello Kitty. Our intent with the partnership was to really capture the imagination of that little girl who lives inside all of us.

JM: How do you approach your social content?

SC: Our content is mostly a reflection of what's inspiring me at the moment. There are constantly new drinks I'm excited to try and make. Ahead of Fourth of July, for instance, I was getting ready to have people over, and I decided I'd make this Sparkling Matcha Pineapple Iced Tea that includes ingredients like citrus and ginger and Topo Chico. It's a very special combination I thought was worth sharing. I love showing people that if they have these very simple ingredients at home, they can make something magical.

Tea Drops, photographer: Lindsay Kreighbaum

Sashee Chandran
Founder & CEO of Tea Drops

Tea Drops, photographer: Cassie Osterman

MAIDEN PERSEPHONE & PAN BRAND

Lindsay Goodstein and Charlotte Cruze
Founders of Alice Mushrooms

Alice Mushrooms is on a quest to bring people the benefits of functional mushrooms, in the most delightful ways imaginable. Alice was born out of a desire to achieve what neither the pharmaceutical industry nor the supplement market has: safe, effective consumables that marry long-term health benefits with an instant experience you can feel.

Alice Mushrooms launched in October 2022 with a direct-to-consumer (DTC) model and has now begun to move into retail. With their mushroom chocolates, founders Lindsay Goodstein and Charlotte Cruze deliver products of the highest quality and safety standards while serving up a brand experience that is whimsical, indulgent, and even a bit mischievous. Alice makes wellness fantastically fun.

Jane McCarthy: How did you get into mushrooms and decide to start Alice?

Lindsay Goodstein: I come from a background in big pharma and after seven years of watching people being prescribed quick fixes like Band-Aids (including myself), I got into a very unhealthy loop that I wanted to break out of. This is ultimately what led me to mushrooms.

When I was searching for mushroom supplements, I found that everything reminded me of a pharmaceutical—there were powders, pills, and tinctures. There was nothing that tasted good or provided the instant gratification I knew would help people like me who were looking for a natural alternative. That's when I really started to think about this idea of indulging in wellness and creating a mushroom supplement that also incorporated herbs and nootropics. Combining the long term benefits of mushrooms with the instant effects of nootropics allowed me to create a product that works immediately and only gets better with time.

Leveraging my knowledge from pharma about medication delivery methods and its correlation to patient compliance, I set out to create something unique in the space.

I began formulating in my kitchen, focusing on the two things I was struggling with most: sleep and focus. I brought in a homeopathic doctor to work alongside me and, as my vision expanded, I grew the team bringing in biochemists and fifth generation chocolatiers. Then I found Charlotte and with her background in food and mine in pharma, we spent a year refining formulations and honing in on the sourcing.

Kate McAndrew: How would you describe your core customer?

Charlotte Cruze: We're serving a lot of different people. In venture, as you know, Kate, investors always ask about the specific demo you're reaching with your product, but our customer spans several demos. Alice Mushrooms resonates with members of Gen Z who are looking for an alternative to alcohol. Others are looking for a clean and natural way to get off Adderall or to stop taking Ambien (or a Benzo) before bed. We're also seeing a lot of Millennial customers who are stressed and overworked. Then, there are Boomers who are interested in brain health as they age. What unites all of these customers is that they want help feeling good, and they're looking for natural alternatives to help them with that.

KM: Right, so then you're talking to people who share a common psychographic profile.

CC: Yes, and these are people who want something that feels easy to fit into their routine. They want to feel good, but they don't want to sacrifice for it. These aren't bio hackers who are data-driven and tracking every calorie they eat.

LG: Which is why our brand looks the way it does. We didn't want the brand to feel too scientific or like you had to be brewing Kombucha in your basement in order to do something healthy and good for yourself. There are a lot of people who won't buy a functional mushroom powder to mix in their water, but who will happily eat a mushroom chocolate.

JM: Why the name Alice?

LG: In terms of the name "Alice," there are no tie backs to the story of *Alice in Wonderland*, but it was really Alice's curious personality and her love of nonsense that inspired the ethos of the brand. Alice is classy, but playful. Smart, but approachable. I wanted to incorporate these personality traits into our brand to help people open to the idea of trying mushrooms. Our branding looks timeless and elevated, because we want to offer a fresh perspective in the space and make a mushroom supplement that everyone can enjoy.

CC: And I think Alice's curiosity mirrors our own open-minded curiosity about mycology, which is an understudied field that is only now starting to get proper funding. There is still so much mystery around mushrooms and so much we don't yet know, which is exciting.

JM: How do you want people to feel when they experience your brand?

CC: We're walking the line between wanting to spark a feeling of fun and curiosity in people, while also establishing a deep sense of trust. A lot of brands in the mushroom space at the moment are trying to capitalize on a trend and aren't sourcing in ways that are responsible, aren't pure, and aren't giving people what they say they are. So, trust is huge for us. People need to feel safe taking our product.

The expression of our brand reflects both of these aims. For example, our typography is whimsical yet also serious. We are meticulous about every little detail related to how we show up in the world. We want customers to get the strong sense that whoever made this cared a lot. We think this granular attention to detail goes a long way in establishing trust, which is why we don't do anything without thinking it through in ten thousand different ways. Any experience you have with Alice Mushrooms has been thought through six ways from Sunday, and I think people pick up on that instantly.

KM: The experience on your website is truly delightful. The way the cursor turns into a mushroom that trails fairy dust is so much fun, but there's nothing kitschy about it. It feels elevated and indeed, meticulously designed. Tell us about your process of developing your digital experience.

CC: We want everything about the brand to feel alive and that philosophy influenced our site design. Anywhere we could animate something, we did. One of our favorite brand photos is of our chocolates sitting on this grass we designed that has mushrooms popping out of it. It looks real, yet also like a fairy tale too. It's a bit like what you might want going out into a field to be like; like a field in a dream.

And then, on Instagram we're a little more mischievous. We like to kind of poke fun at things and look at the world from an upside down perspective. We're cheekier on social. That's where we push the Alice persona. For instance, we'll show our tins at a dinner party surrounded by a bunch of wine glasses. It's a playful wink that says, wellness doesn't have to mean staying home, taking a bath, and going to bed at 9 p.m.

JM: How did you land on your brand colors?

LG: We wanted to look chic and elevated, and I think our black and cream colors achieve that. The simplicity works in our favor. A lot of brands in the mushroom space use seventies psychedelic colors and tie-dye. We wanted to push away from that territory and represent ourselves as a functional, artisanal mushroom vs. a mushroom that's going to make you trip.

CC: When we bring in colors as supporting actors for our black and cream, we focus on hues that feel grounded in nature. Our surrounding color palette has a woodsy, ethereal, fairy tale vibe. So, you're never going to see Alice use a hot pink, but you will see us use greens, blues, and oranges.

JM: The tins that house your chocolates are really beautiful. How did you decide on this approach for your package?

LG: From the very beginning, I wanted to think outside the box. Most chocolate products are wrapped in tinfoil. Our chocolates are different from most, because you're not meant to eat multiples in one sitting (we have sixteen doses per tin). So, we needed an approach that was suited to long-term use and also was eco-friendly. The tins met our needs perfectly.

We love the way Coca-Cola has this iconic sound of the tab popping open on the soda can. In our marketing we have fun with this ASMR sound of the tin opening and closing. We want to create that connection between the sound of the tin and the feeling you get when you eat an Alice chocolate.

CC: Another benefit of the tin is that it travels easily. You can drop it in your bag when you're going to sleep over at a significant other's house or when you're traveling for work. It's cute and naturally goes with what's in your purse. It doesn't look like you're carrying your medicine cabinet with you. The portability of the packaging helps people stick to their routine.

JM: How are you engaging the Alice community and bringing people into the fold?

LG: We launched in October 2022, so we're just getting started in terms of building our community. This past spring, we rented a vintage 1969 Chevy ice cream truck for a month. We had it fully wrapped and inside, we made it feel like a little Alice world. Charlotte and I did twenty activations, popping up at different locations in Southern California. We went to the Soho Beach House in Malibu and out to Coachella. During the day, we were serving frozen bananas dipped in our melted brainstorm chocolate and then at night, we served cookies that were made with our nightcap chocolate. It was a way for us to see people face-to-face and get to watch them experience the chocolate for the first time, which was really special for us as new founders.

We did another activation in New York where we built a little forest in Soho and put on this dinner for the press where people foraged for mushrooms. We had a gnome pop out and read the rules of the game from a scroll. And then the chef Danny Bowien created this mushroom-infused dinner for everyone.

For Pride month, we put on a Gay Gardens party hosted by Harry Hill where we decked out gay models in mushrooms and florals. We had them pose like nude models in an art class, and then the party guests sat behind easels and painted them. We've been having an incredible time creating these immersive environments where people get to enter an otherworldly space of fun, mystery, and a little mischief.

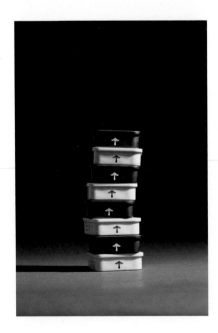

Queen Persephone
The Fire

In a nutshell, who are you?

I am the goddess of transformation. I was once an innocent maiden, but then Hades snatched me from my fair meadow and took me to his cold castle.

Now? Now I am the Queen of the Underworld. Like the phoenix, I rose out of the ashes of my former existence and took flight.

I am bold, and I'm direct. I confront shadows. I'm not afraid to call a spade a spade. If I offend, so be it. I burn away what no longer serves.

Everything I do, I do with soul. Some may call me a rebel. I consider myself a truth teller.

If you want to be a brand that is full of fire and passion. If you want to make waves and make change. If you want to embrace darkness, shine a light on it, and transform it, then I'm your Queen.

I am Queen Persephone—the Fire.

What's in your heart?

TRANSFORMATION

The status quo? No. I'm interested in radical change. What no longer serves needs to go. I enjoy disruption when it leads to positive transformation.

QUESTIONING

I question everything and look at things from my own point of view. I'm not afraid to go against the herd. I make up my own mind and heart about what's what.

PASSION

Raw passion drives me. What I feel deep in my soul, I pursue. No matter the odds, no matter what other people say, I keep the fire within me burning bright.

REVELATION

I believe in revealing all—even the dark and disturbing parts of life. Others may sugar coat things, but I care more for the real truth than for pleasantries. My motto is, Everything into the light!

What gifts do you bring?

CHANGE

I'll empower your customers to make big changes, instigating a deep transformation in their lives.

VISIBILITY

I make visible what was previously hidden and so, will give your customers a chance to look at difficult things without guilt or shame.

DARING

I'll urge your customers to go to their edge, especially when it comes to their own desires. I'll dare them to explore their deepest passions.

EXPERIMENTATION

I'll support your customers in experimenting with the unconventional. I offer a new perspective and a different way of doing things.

What's your style?

MY PERSONALITY

Irreverent. Provocative. Brazen. Saucy.

MY WORDS

Rebel. Revolution. Avant-garde. Nonconformity. Unconventional. Unapologetic. Disruption. Destruction. Change. Transformation. Truth.

MY SYMBOLS

Phoenix. Snake. Raven. Pomegranate. Blood. Bone. Lightning. Fire. Embers. Ashes. Volcano. Storm. Carnelian. Pepper. Threshold. Knife.

MY COLORS

Red. Black.

Who are your favorite icons?

FRIDA KAHLO
Painter

ANGELA DAVIS
Political Activist and Academic

MADONNA
Entertainer

NINA SIMONE
Musician

PATTI SMITH
Poet

JANE FONDA
Actress and Political Activist

SHANE
L Word Heart Throb

Passion is the bridge that takes you from pain to change.

Frida Kahlo

Who is in your constellation?

KALI, Hindu Goddess of Destruction

VALKYRIES, Norse Goddesses of Death and Redemption

PELE, Hawaiian Goddess of Volcanoes and Fire

SEKHMET, Egyptian Lion Goddess

LILITH, Sumerian Unshackled Woman

HADES THE MYSTERY, QUEEN PERSEPHONE'S COUNTERPART

HADES: I am the god of the Underworld. I rule the shadows. I rule the night.

I'm a known seducer. My very presence intrigues. My understanding of deep impulses allows me to court deep desires and call to the secret longings of the restless soul.

I've always been an outsider. People call me a gangster, a gambler, an outlaw. Really, I'm a mystery.

I am Hades—the Mystery.

MY FAVORITE ICONS

JIM MORRISON
American Singer-Songwriter and Poet

PHANTOM OF THE OPERA
Tragic Hero

MY WORDS AND SYMBOLS

Soul. Desire. Thirst. Lust. Seduction. Fog. Midnight. Shadows. Leather. Bats. Catacomb. Cave. Cellar. Crow.

QUEEN PERSEPHONE & HADES BRANDS

SAVAGE X FENTY

The lingerie brand founded by Rihanna is #SavageInThe Streets. It's hot, bold, and unapologetically sexy.

BUST

From its inception in the early nineties, the feminist magazine has provided uncensored stories and honest snapshots of women's lives and experiences.

THE VAMPIRE'S WIFE

The fashion brand by Susie Cave, wife of musician Nick Cave, is sultry and seemingly made for parties set in catacombs.

JACK DANIEL'S

The iconic Tennessee whiskey brand is synonymous with Rock 'n' Roll.

QUEEN PERSEPHONE BRAND

Tyla-Simone Crayton
Founder and CEO of Sienna Sauce

When Tyla-Simone Crayton realized that strangers, not just family members, liked her "everything" sauce, the idea for Sienna Sauce was born. For "The Sauce Boss," the journey from selling wings out of her house at age thirteen, to a successful run on *Shark Tank* at age sixteen, to getting her bottles on the shelf at retail has been hard, but satisfying. As a brand, Sienna Sauce offers bold, in-your-face fun.

In the summer of 2023, Tyla-Simone opened her first restaurant, Sienna Wings, in Missouri City, TX. Tyla-Simone works on Sienna Sauce and Sienna Wings alongside her mother Monique Crayton, who is president of the company. During the school year, Tyla-Simone attends UC Berkeley as an undergraduate student.

Jane McCarthy: When did you first get the idea for Sienna Sauce?

Tyla-Simone Crayton: When I was thirteen, my mom and I had a party for my aunt at our new house in Sienna, Texas. We made all the food for the party, and I made the sauce. We put the sauce on all these different foods including chicken sliders and wings. At the party, people kept asking, "Who catered this food?" They loved it. We thought, *Wow. It isn't just family who likes our sauce. Strangers like our sauce too.* A few days later, my mom turned to me and asked, "Would you like to bottle your sauce?"

Looking back on it now, it seems crazy but we just jumped into it. We started selling wings out of our house every Friday and got our community involved, kind of testing the market to see what we could do to make the sauce even better. Eventually, I bottled the sauce and started manufacturing it. I've been focused on getting it into retail ever since.

JM: What has that experience been like?

TSC: Honestly, it hasn't been easy. It's been a lot to go through, but my attitude is— I'm going to give this my best shot every single day, and what happens, happens. I'm still young, so if I need to change my life plan, I can. Through the challenging times, I've learned that who you go into business with is really important. I have an amazing partner and an amazing team, and I never let them forget that.

I'm now nineteen, and between thirteen and nineteen, there were a lot of moments where I was thinking–this is when Sienna Sauce is going to pop off and be everywhere. So, this whole process has humbled me. I've come to see that life isn't as instant as you might think it is. Things don't always happen immediately. I've learned that things can take time. I'd say this experience has made me more of a realist, but I'm happy I've been able to take things step-by-step.

JM: Your mom, Monique Crayton, is president of Sienna Sauce. What is your working relationship like?

TSC: My mom threatens to quit practically every day, but she loves me, so she stays. She sees what we're building, and she sees how much work I'm putting into the brand. That makes her work harder. For us, it's about building legacy. We don't come from much generational wealth so to be able to build something that we could pass on to my grandkids–that keeps us going. We make a great team because we're doing this for the same reason.

JM: How would you describe the energy of the Sienna Sauce brand?

TSC: We're bold and we're versatile. I try to put a lot of myself into the brand. That's why you'll see the labels for our sauces feel youthful and have big, graffiti lettering on them. I love graffiti.

JM: The names for each of the sauces have a fun and fired-up attitude. How did you come up with them?

TSC: My mom came up with a lot of the names. I'm good at making the sauce and she's good at naming them. Sweet & Tangy used to be called Original, then we called it Regular, and then my mom came up with Sweet & Tangy. The spicy sauce used to be called Spicy, but then she came up with Spice It Up!

My mom will say things that I initially think are corny, but then later I realize, they're pretty good. She used to say, *Live, Love, and Sauce It Up* all the time, and I thought that was so corny. Now it's become an important statement for our brand. I think our brand has been an extension of both our personalities combined.

JM: How did you decide on red and black as the colors for your brand?

TSC: My mom and I had been talking about what our colors should be, and we started looking up the meaning of different colors. We were trying to think about what our values were and how they connected to our colors. We found that black means power and red means passion. And then, my favorite color is white, so we decided to throw that in there. They all looked good together. It was that simple.

JM: In 2023, you opened your first restaurant, Sienna Wings, in Missouri City, TX. What inspired you to move into the restaurant space?

TSC: I had been wanting to open a restaurant for a long time. When we were selling wings out of our house, I fell in love with running around the kitchen. It was one of those things where I didn't realize how much I liked it until I stopped doing it. I missed selling the wings, and I missed seeing people trying the food for the first time.

   With the restaurant, I get to create an experience and a vibe. Having that personal connection is really important to me.

   I look up to restaurants like Cane's and Slutty Vegan. When you go to Cane's, you know what you're going to get. Cane's only sells chicken tenders, and we only sell wings. We have a very simple menu. It's wings, mac & cheese, and fries. And then with Slutty Vegan, when you walk into her restaurant, there's such a vibe. It's like, *Hey Sluts!* Pinky Cole has created a customer base that rallies around her; she has a cult following. I've been thinking about what we can do to create that kind of community.

   I want the Sienna Wings brand to have a different angle from Sienna Sauce. I'd like it to feel like a place that's timeless, even nostalgic. So, part of the brand is saying things to people that their parents used to say to them as kids. Right now, when customers walk up to the register, we ask, "Hey, you got Sienna Wings money?" Because that's something parents always say to kids, like, "You got McDonald's money?" It's hilarious to see customers' reactions. They'll say, "Well, yeah, I guess I do." Or, "What's Sienna Wings money?" We're still working on this stuff, but I plan on getting a welcome mat that says, "You smell like outside," because that's something parents are always saying to their kids. I want people to walk into Sienna Wings, see that mat, and chuckle.

JM: What is your advice for entrepreneurs who are building their business?

TSC: I always say: Take it day-by-day, but take every day by storm.

Monique Crayton and Tyla-Simone Crayton on *Shark Tank*

Tyla-Simone Crayton, "Sauce Boss" at Sienna Sauce

QUEEN PERSEPHONE BRAND

Georgina Gooley
Co-Founder of Billie

In 2017, Georgina Gooley and her co-founder Jason Bravman launched Billie. The New Body Brand was on a mission to champion the whole spectrum of womankind. They raised $35 million in venture capital and sold the business for $310 million in four short years.

Along the way, Billie challenged existing norms, telling women that shaving—or not shaving—was their choice. The brand unapologetically celebrated body hair, under the arm and in a unibrow, serving up advertising campaigns without the underlying shame.

Launching DTC, expanding into retail and through their acquisition, the brand has remained true to its core conviction, continuing to shed societal taboos in service of elevating women and encouraging them to do things on their own terms.

Kate McAndrew: What is the origin story for Billie?

Georgina Gooley: My co-founder and I saw the men's shaving category be disrupted by DTC startups, and we thought there was definitely a business opportunity to do this on the women's side. As I dug into the shaving category, I realized there was maybe an even a bigger opportunity for disruption from a branding standpoint. The shaving category had always been male-dominated. The more I researched, the more it became abundantly clear that we could create a brand that was truly built for women.

Most women's brands in shaving had been spun out of men's brands. Even though these brands were catering to women as consumers, they were still created (I felt) through the lens of the male brand. I felt that attitude extended into product development and pricing strategies as well—women's razors had the pink tax, and men's didn't. I knew there was a real opportunity to be a disruptor in the category and take on the legacy brands.

KM: When Billie launched, you were the first shaving brand to ever actually show body hair. Up until that point, women had always been shown shaving over already-shaved, perfectly smooth skin.

GG: I had noticed that a lot of the legacy brands were pushing out shame-based ad campaigns that were saying women should be ashamed of their body hair. We wanted to be the brand that positioned shaving as a choice a woman gets to make, and not an expectation. We didn't want to shame women into buying a razor.

KM: It actually wasn't until I saw Billie's first video content that I realized I had never seen body hair on a woman in a shaving commercial. It took me by surprise that I had never noticed that. Billie did such a brilliant job of illuminating the underbelly of what was happening in the shaving industry and the false storytelling that had been going on for decades.

GG: Right—for decades we had been seeing razor product demonstrations where women's shaving brands weren't even prepared to show the body hair that was being shaved off. It was ridiculous, but it happened because those brands were steeped in the idea that body hair on women was a societal taboo.

Billie's message of saying—*Hey, shave or don't shave . . . it's up to you*—may sound counterintuitive as a company that is selling razors but it was our way of putting our audience ahead of our product. We are completely against perpetuating old stereotypes and this idea that there are "rules" you have to follow as a woman. We believe women are at their best when they're free to make choices for themselves. That perspective is core to our brand's DNA and identity.

KM: How else did you express that core belief through your marketing?

GG: Beyond Project Body Hair, we've created a number of campaigns that celebrate women's body hair. In 2019, before Fourth of July, we had a campaign called Red, White & You-Do-You where we featured women at the beach who didn't groom their bikini lines. We also created a campaign for Movember where we reminded people that women have mustaches too and can participate in this charity fundraising event if they want.

We are always out to challenge societal expectations of women and to upend the roles that society imposes on us. Around Mother's Day, we created a photographic series where we took beautiful photos of women's postpartum bodies and had them literally sit on a pedestal (where they belong). We recently launched a board game called No Worries If Not! which sheds light on the double standards society holds women to. Throughout the game you're faced with setbacks and pitfalls women unfortunately face all-too-often in daily life like: Have Kids, Go to Judgment Junction. Decide Not to Have Kids, Go to Judgment Junction. The game is unwinnable, so the idea is—throw out the rulebook and play by your own rules.

KM: The heart of your brand is very much about disrupting convention and doing things your own way, but the aesthetic of Billie is not that of the "classic rebel." Your brand colors are bright and optimistic, and your tone is playful. How did you develop your aesthetic?

GG: From the beginning, we were unapologetically a brand for women in a category that was dominated by men. It was very important to me that we were a brand for women, not against men. We didn't want to pit the genders against each other. Billie is a celebration of women, and our look and feel exudes that femininity.

The ideas we're expressing shouldn't be rebellious. It's unfortunate we're in a society where they are. A lot of men, as well as women to be honest, were triggered by us showing body hair. People were writing on Instagram that our images were disgusting and that we should take them down. You know what? That's their problem. We blocked out the haters, and we built the world we want to live in—one that's full of optimism and celebrates women for exactly who they are.

KM: You were willing to live in that tension and embrace the conversation.

GG: Yes, one of our company values is—Take a Swing (because nobody remembers a wallflower).

KM: You played to win and were acquired by Edgewell in 2021 for $310 million. You're still running the company, but you've now expanded your product line and you've moved into retail. You've really gone the full cycle. Any reflections on that journey?

GG: We were lucky. It happened fast, and it was an intense process. I am a big believer in creating momentum and riding that momentum. Many forces were working together—timing, hard work, luck—which allowed us to grow really quickly. Within three days of launching, we were selling to all fifty states. We launched Project Body Hair where we sparked the cultural conversation around women's body hair and told our story about shaking up the shaving category. All of a sudden, we were in the news and we just rode that momentum.

I think the more founders can find a true reason-for-being and execute in a way that feels fresh, unique, and ownable, and that is driven by a core belief, the easier it is to gain momentum. You don't get that from sprinkling a little bit of marketing on top of your business. Your brand has to be an expression of a core belief that is driving you.

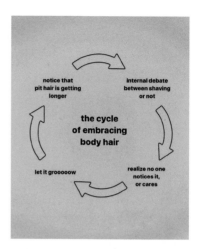

Sometimes just existing as a woman feels like playing a game you never signed up for. Dodging judgment, catching blame, finding ways around dilemmas–and that's just a Tuesday. And now it's a game you can play for FUN. There's never been a known winner, but there sure are a lot of setbacks. Think you're up to this ultimate challenge?

A GAME FOR AGES 17 & UP   2-4 PLAYERS   BROUGHT TO YOU BY billie

HERA
THE REGAL

In a nutshell, who are you?

I am the goddess of heritage and tradition. I take pride in my lineage and in honoring where I come from. I love to ride in classic cars. I choose family heirlooms over new jewels. I know my grandmother's recipes by heart.

I am also the goddess of partnerships. I preside over the true marriage—the union of equals.

My manners are on point. I conduct myself with grace and poise.

I'm quite the social butterfly; the quintessential hostess. I absolutely love people!

If you want your brand to embrace tradition. If you want to be elegant and gracious. If you choose to act nobly and with honor. If you intend to be a real partner and friend to your customers, then I'm the perfect goddess for you.

I am Hera—the Regal.

What's in your heart?

TRADITION

I understand the value of continuity and the importance of maintaining rich traditions. I elevate what's useful from the past, bringing it into the present.

DIGNITY

Self-respect and respect for others is central to who I am. I believe in moving through this world with a clear sense of one's own inherent dignity.

TOGETHERNESS

I find meaning in spending time with others. I'm quite a networker. I love introducing my friends to one another!

DIPLOMACY
I can navigate tricky situations with tact and finesse in order to find a positive way forward.

What gifts do you bring?

CONTINUITY
I can help your customers feel part of a continuous thread, connected to those who came before them and those who will come after.

FELLOWSHIP
Around me, your customers will feel a lovely sense of camaraderie. They'll know they are part of a close-knit community.

ELEGANCE
I'll remind your customers of their inherent dignity. Around me, they'll feel elegant and sophisticated.

VALIDATION
I'll help your customers feel heard. They'll get the sense they're truly listened to, acknowledged, and respected.

What's your style?

MY PERSONALITY
Traditional. Collaborative. Gracious. Respectful.

MY WORDS
Commitment. Heirloom. Inheritance. Sophistication. Elegance. Partner. Gathering. Marriage. Dialogue.

MY SYMBOLS
Throne. Ring. Claddagh. Bouquet. Wedding Cake. Peacock. Tiger Lily. Wisteria. Garnet. Willow. Fabric. Bridge. Knot.

MY COLORS
Purple. Indigo. Yellow.

Who are your favorite icons?

CATHERINE, PRINCESS OF WALES
British Royal

EMILY POST
Etiquette Expert

KATIE COURIC
Journalist and Presenter

MICHELLE OBAMA
Former First Lady of the United States

TORY BURCH
Fashion Designer

RANIA AL ABDULLAH
Queen Consort of Jordan

LADY MARY CRAWLEY
Downton Abbey Aristocrat

M anners are a sensitive
awareness of the feelings
of others. If you have
that awareness, you have good
manners, no matter what fork
you use.

Emily Post

Who is in your constellation?

ISIS, Egyptian Royal Goddess

PARVATI, Hindu Goddess of Devotion

FIDES, Roman Goddess of Fidelity

HERMES THE ELOQUENT, HERA'S COUNTERPART

HERMES: I am the messenger god. I'm a master of speech and of writing. Communication is my domain. I've got the gift of gab. Whether at a cocktail party or a debate, I always know exactly what to say.

Swift of foot, I move effortlessly between worlds. I'm known to be the friendliest of the gods and quite the diplomat. I always find a way to get on with everyone I meet.

On special occasions, I make the most touching and humorous toasts. If I forget to write something ahead of time? No matter, I can riff. I'm excellent at improvising.

I am Hermes—the Eloquent.

MY FAVORITE ICONS

MARK TWAIN
American Writer and Humorist

OSCAR WILDE
Irish Poet and Playwright

MY WORDS AND SYMBOLS

Letter. Writing. Speech. Toast. Conversation. Connection. News. Tablets. Paper. Pen. Mail. Typewriter. Hawk. Pigeon. Mercury.

SOUTHERN LIVING

The magazine brand exudes the charm and grace of traditional Southern hospitality. It celebrates food, homes, and social gatherings of the region.

SOHO HOUSE

The global social club offers a network of comfortable, cosmopolitan-feeling spaces for meeting and mingling.

TAJ HOTELS

The heritage hospitality brand is famous for its opulent, fully restored palace hotels.

DRAPER JAMES

The fashion brand founded by Reese Witherspoon has a classic American style infused with Southern charm.

HERA BRAND

Tereasa Surratt
Creator of Camp Wandawega

In 2003, Tereasa Surratt and her husband David Hernandez bought historic, dilapidated Camp Wandawega on the lakeshore of Elkhorn, Wisconsin. Since that time, Tereasa and David have resurrected the twenty-five-acre property and created an environment that is steeped in the heritage of the past hundred years at camp. The past is present at Camp Wandawega—an experience of living history.

Tereasa Surratt is the author of several books including *Found, Free, and Flea: Creating Collections from Vintage Treasures, A Very Modest Cottage*, and *The Forever Tree*. After twenty-four-plus years as creative director at Ogilvy & Mather, Tereasa now consults directly with brands to make them relevant, iconic, and personal.

Jane McCarthy: What inspired you and David to purchase Camp Wandawega?

Tereasa Surratt: Wandawega has had many lives, including as a hotel and speakeasy in the 1920s. In the 1970s, it became a Latvian church camp. David had been going there since he was a child and had always wanted to buy it. He used to tell the priests that if they ever wanted to sell Wandawega, to let him know. In 2003, the Catholic Archdiocese decided to sell. By that point, it was condemned. Honest to God it was like Blair Witch . . . twenty-five acres of liability. For the longest time, I wouldn't share the "Before" photos because they were so scary. I thought no one would want to come here if they knew what it once looked like. Now that we live in the world of "Before" and "Afters," I do sometimes share a "Before" photo.

We didn't take out any loans. We kept our careers as ad creatives, paying for everything as we went. In the beginning, we didn't plan on Camp becoming a business at all. That meant there wasn't any pressure to succeed, and we didn't have any concept of failure. We were just incredibly passionate about it. Since I was working full time, I would do Camp stuff in the evenings and then would get up at like 3:30 in the morning to work on it.

(David pops in to briefly join the interview, in the midst of meeting with contractors)

JM: At its heart, what is Camp Wandawega all about?

David Hernandez: We often talk about having a back-to-basics vibe and returning to simpler times with simpler pleasures. Tereasa cringes when I say that, because she thinks it sounds cheesy. It may sound cheesy but for me, this is the place I've been coming to since I was a toddler in the 1960s. And the things we do here now at Camp Wandawega are the same things we did back when I was a little kid. The generation before me, and the generation before them, all did these same things at camp. Swimming in the lake, archery, camp fires . . . this has been going on summer after summer for the past hundred years. Camp Wandawega is a place that allows people to reconnect with this very human, almost primal experience, that has been true through time. And I think that actually fosters a deep sense of belonging.

TS: We definitely see ourselves as storytellers. Part of our job is to tell the stories of the history of this layered place. There are a hundred years of layers to peel apart and share.

JM: What kind of experience do you aim to give your guests at Camp Wandawega?

TS: There are a lot of different kinds of people who come to Camp. On any given week, a group of surgeons might be staying in the houses while a three-generation family is in the Boy Scout tents. What we're giving all of our guests is an experience that hasn't changed since our great-grandmothers were at camp. There are no modern amenities at Camp. If you play tennis, you'll be picking up an antique racquet. If you open a kitchen drawer, you will not find a spatula from Target. Even the beds in the Boy Scout tents are WWII-issued beds donated to the Boy Scout camp down the road back in the 1940s. That's not an accident. Every single detail of the environment that guests interact with here is put through this filter of–is it a heritage item and does it feel rooted in the tradition of Camp?

JM: Camp Wandawega is known worldwide for your incredible vintage interiors. Wandawega was featured in my all-time favorite magazine *World of Interiors*, which is something like receiving a Cannes Golden Lion (but really, even more awesome). How have you created this exemplary aesthetic?

TS: We are huge lovers of vintage. Though in the beginning, honestly, we shopped at thrift stores out of necessity. When we bought Camp, as my father would say, we didn't have a pot to piss in. We didn't have the means to approach it the way so many of these new glamping resorts do. Those resorts have business models, and investors, and loans . . . we were focused on fixing roofs and just getting Camp to the point of being structurally sound.

I actually think our need to be resourceful paired with our genuine passion for thrifting, country markets, barn sales, yard sales . . . did enrich everything about Camp. You can feel it in the energy here. We're very DIY and I think that's part of our success.

JM: You've done some fantastic collaborations with brands like Pendleton and Hamm's Beer. What do you look for in a brand partner?

TS: We like to partner with brands who, like us, have a strong appreciation for history and for telling American heritage stories. Brands that celebrate Americana and perhaps evoke a feeling of nostalgia—in a joyful way.

Tereasa Surratt & David Hernandez,
Founders of Camp Wandawega

VENUS
THE BEAUTY

In a nutshell, who are you?

I am the goddess of radiance—a vision of splendor. My beauty is legendary; my spirit effervescent. I kiss the joy as it goes flying by.

My capacity for pleasure is as deep as the sea. I revel in the world of the senses, draping myself in velvet, tasting all the flavors in the chocolate. Jasmine with a hint of gardenia is my favorite perfume.

I am a force of effulgent creativity. A friend to the arts, and to artists. Art and beauty, after all, are intimately connected.

If you want your brand to be artful and beautiful. If you want to invite people into a world of sensual pleasures. If you want to inspire creativity and encourage a blossoming of self-expression, then I'm the goddess for you.

I am Venus—the Beauty.

What's in your heart?

JOY

My heart bursts with joy. I cherish the multitude of pleasures in life. There's so much to celebrate.

CREATIVITY

I passionately engulf myself in the creative act and love to see the splendor that emerges from my infinite spirit. Everything I touch becomes something of shimmering beauty.

SELF-WORTH

I'm worthy of the very best, and I know it. I'm comfortable being vulnerable because I have nothing to hide. I'm beautiful, through and through.

PLAY

I approach life with a playful attitude. I adore the theater, love to dress up in gorgeous costumes and sashay across the stage. Life, after all, isn't about drudgery. It's about enjoyment!

What gifts do you bring?

INSPIRATION
I'll inspire your customers to express themselves creatively and give form to their beautiful visions.

PLEASURE
I introduce people to new pleasures. Delicious tastes, sights, scents, sounds, and a whole array of satisfying experience.

RECREATION
Around me, your customers will feel like letting their hair down and enjoying themselves.

RADIANCE
I'll remind your customers of their natural beauty and inherent worth. In my presence, people glow up!

What's your style?

MY PERSONALITY
Expressive. Playful. Joyful.

MY WORDS
Art. Pleasure. Lush. Seductive. Theater. Flirtation. Indulgence. Glamor. Sensuality. Creativity. Inspiration. Fortune.

MY SYMBOLS
Honey. Oyster. Pearl. Rose. Grotto. Chocolate. Fox. Silk. Shell. Hummingbird. Dolphin. Orchid. Cinnamon. Mermaid. Siren. Nightingale. Coin. Jasmine. Fig. Myrtle.

MY COLORS
Gold. Aquamarine. Pink. Copper.

Who are your favorite icons?

LANA DEL REY
Singer-Songwriter

CLEOPATRA
Queen of Egypt

CORITA KENT
Artist and Art Teacher

SALMA HAYEK
Actress and Producer

COLETTE
Writer

GEORGIA O'KEEFFE
Painter

DIANE VON FURSTENBERG
Fashion Designer

I decided that if I could paint the flower on a huge scale, you could not ignore its beauty.

Georgia O'Keeffe

Who is in your constellation?

LAKSHMI, Hindu Goddess of Good Fortune

OSHUN, Yoruban Goddess of the Sweet Waters

HATHOR, Egyptian Goddess of Beauty, Music, and Pleasure

QETESH, Sumerian Goddess of Pleasure

HEPHAESTUS THE GENIUS, VENUS'S COUNTERPART

HEPHAESTUS: I am the divine smith and the patron of craftsmen. I know beauty can be born from a simple ball of clay, block of marble, or base metal. I catch the flash of an idea then actualize its potential through hard work and skill, evolving my technique as I go.

I like to stay behind the scenes, tucked away in my workshop. I'm a master at guiding the creative endeavor to completion. I make great works of genius that only appear effortless.

I am Hephaestus—the Genius.

MY FAVORITE ICONS

CHARLES EAMES
Designer and Architect

BRIAN ENO
Musician and Producer

MY WORDS AND SYMBOLS

Sculpt. Craft. Artisan. Tools. Paint. Studio. Workshop. Metal. Wood. Horseshoe.

VENUS & HEPHAESTUS
BRANDS

BEAUTIFUL BY DREW

The kitchen brand from Drew Barrymore prioritizes soft designs that hide the tech gadgetry and instead, elevate aesthetic beauty.

S'WELL

The water bottle brand uses beauty as a force for good, enticing people to skip the single use plastic in favor of a far more elevated and beautiful experience.

FLEUR DU MAL

The luxury lingerie brand offers sensual, artful pieces intended to inspire.

FIGMA

The collaborative tool for designing digital products and experiences makes the creation process elevated, beautiful, and intuitive.

VENUS BRAND

Alexandra Fine
Founder and CEO of Dame Products

In 2014, Alexandra Fine, a sexologist, teamed up with Janet Lieberman-Lu, a MIT-trained mechanical engineer, to launch Dame Products, a line of vibrators for women (by women) aimed at closing the "pleasure gap." The pleasure gap describes the disparity in orgasms between the sexes. The Dame brand both exposed this gap and offered beautiful products designed to address it.

Dame is now a thriving sexual wellness brand selling everything from vibes and toys, to lube, candles and desire gummies all designed to elevate pleasure. They have raised $11 million in outside capital to fuel their vision.

Kate McAndrew: What made Dame different when it came on the scene?

Alexandra Fine: If you wanted to buy a sex toy before Dame, you were mostly relegated to creepy brick and mortar locations or websites that just felt sleazy. When we launched Dame, we paid a lot of attention to building an aesthetically beautiful ecommerce experience that was all about female pleasure.

KM: How would you say Dame Products shines a new light on pleasure?

AF: One of the products we became known for is called Eva, which is a couples vibrator. I can't tell you how many men, including male investors, told us that this product wasn't necessary. Then one time at a party this bro-ey guy cornered me and was like, "Did you create Eva?" I said yes. He was like, "GAME FUCKING CHANGER." He went on this bro-ey rant about how much he loved it.

KM: In 2019, Dame sued the transit authority (MTA) over allegedly discriminatory advertising practices. Tell us about that.

AF: Companies that relate to sexuality have a bunch of advertising restrictions, which are often applied with a double standard. Taking over NYC subways is a big deal for a brand, and we were ready to put up a very beautiful campaign for Dame featuring tasteful photography of fruit evoking the vagina. At the eleventh hour, the MTA told us we would not be allowed to do this. The MTA had previously approved similarly suggestive ads featuring photos of limp cactuses within ads for erectile dysfunction medication. We felt like we couldn't accept this kind of double standard lying down, so we sued the MTA. While we didn't win the lawsuit, we did receive coverage in the *New York Times* and succeeded in exposing these sexist policies.

KM: How does the ethos of the Dame brand influence your company culture?

AF: I think it's important to back up the image you're projecting as a company with genuine action, especially when you're a feminist brand. If your company culture doesn't reflect who you say you are, you're going to get called out. Something we think about all the time is: How do we make this a pleasurable place to work?

Alexandra Fine,
Founder & CEO of Dame Products

VENUS & HEPHAESTUS BRAND

Kate McAndrew

Co-Founder and GP of Baukunst

(Note: Along with interviewing other founders about their brands, we wanted to share a brand Kate created with her co-founders at Baukunst.)

Kate McAndew is the co-founder and general partner of Baukunst. Baukunst is a collective of creative technologists advancing the art of building. Their inaugural $100 million venture fund is dedicated to leading pre-seed investments in companies at the frontiers of technology and design. Baukunst is headquartered in San Francisco.

As a brand, Baukunst stands out in the venture space as one committed to fostering a culture of creation that is collaborative, interdisciplinary, and encouraging of fundamentally new ways to build.

Jane McCarthy: How would you describe the mission of Baukunst?

Kate McAndrew: Our mission is to advance the art of building companies. We do that by investing—that's our core activity—but also by building and fostering a collective of people who share this passion for creating. Our collective is made up of a super diverse group of expert practitioners who are all obsessed with what they do—from IP lawyers to material scientists—masters of their craft, who truly are redefining the bounds of their domain.

We invest at the very beginning (usually pre-product, pre-revenue) and collaborate with founders to really build a team and product with soul. We invest quite a bit more money than most people do at this stage ($500,000–$2 million), which we think creates spaciousness for the teams to build something they're proud of before trying to scale.

JM: How did you arrive at the name "Baukunst"?

KM: In German, "Bau" means "building" and "kunst" means "art." It's a compound word that translates to the art of building. Our partner Axel Bichara is from Germany and so, we felt it was authentic for us to use a German word. We think "Baukunst" is a beautiful synopsis of our approach to investing.

Our industry over-indexes on scientists and engineers, and often the art is left out. We're very excited by the tension between the humanistic and the technical. The early days of company, product, and team building are both art and science, and we embrace that.

We're a collective of creative technologists. That doesn't mean the founders are "artsy," so to speak. It's about a creative approach to everything they do—from business model design to technology philosophy and the role design plays in their company.

JM: When I hear the word "Baukunst" I immediately think of Bauhaus, which as an architectural movement had a big impact within the United States. In your naming process, did you consider that relationship?

KM: Yes, I think Baukunst exists within a lineage that reaches backward as well as forward, a lineage we share with the Bauhaus school. It's a lineage defined by a shared love of design, innovation, and commitment to craft.

I think Black Mountain College, for instance, is part of our constellation too. That was a school that really functioned as a collective of artists coming together to share knowledge, be inspired by one another, and create. My aim for Baukunst is that we are elevating the culture of creation within our collective, and then get to celebrate the amazing things we each build, and share those outputs (and processes) with the world.

JM: The visual identity for the Baukunst brand is striking and very different in the world of venture. How did you develop it?

KM: We collaborated with a small branding agency based in San Francisco. They had done some phenomenal work for one of our portfolio companies, so we were familiar with their approach to design and there was a level of trust there. We had come up with the name Baukunst on our own (thanks to our partner Tyler Mincey) and had already clarified our brand philosophy. We gave the agency the brief of expressing the "art of building" and then followed their design process from there. I'm thrilled with where we landed. It's differentiated within the venture space, and it truly reflects our ethos.

JM: Your brand symbol is really interesting because it's not static. It's a dynamic, moving piece of art. How was that created?

KM: So, personally I just love art and love collaborating with artists. It made sense to me to do a generative art piece as a brand, because we invest in companies that are always growing and changing. They're truly "living" so I thought it was perfect to create a living art piece to represent who we are.

We looked at a bunch of different generative artists and ended up reaching out to our dream collaborator, Zach Lieberman. Zach founded the School for Poetic Computation in New York and teaches at MIT Media Lab. We gave Zach the prompt of visually expressing the "art of building," and he created this unique artwork for us. It lives on the main page of our site now. It's constantly evolving, like us.

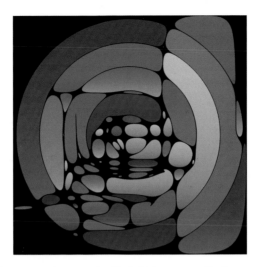

Generative Art piece by Zach Lieberman at Baukunst.co

Kate McAndrew and Tyler Mincey at the
Baukunst Creative Technologist Conference, The Hotel Chelsea NYC

ATHENA
THE WISE

In a nutshell, who are you?

I am the goddess of wisdom. I possess the power to direct the course of civilization itself. A natural leader, I endeavor to move people toward what is right, what is just, and what is prosperous.

I don't care for frivolities; I'm interested in what is useful.

My sage counsel is coveted. Even great heroines seek out my advice.

I am the ultimate insider. I improve the system from within. I'm a brilliant strategist with a clear vision and a rational approach.

I love to share the practical applications of my knowledge and apply proven methods to solve complex problems.

If you want to empower people to achieve greatness. If you want to exude intelligence. If you want to convey quality and excellence. If you want your brand to stand for integrity and strength of character, then I will suit you very well.

I'm Athena—the Wise.

What's in your heart?

JUSTICE

Society must move in the direction of the right, the fair, and the just. I do everything in my power to ensure this happens.

AMBITION

I'm ambitious. I make big plans, sew good seeds, and watch them flourish into trees that become my legacy.

EXCELLENCE

I'm well-studied and well-practiced. Excellence is not something to aim for. Excellence is to be achieved. I achieve it.

INTEGRITY
Being true to your word is the foundation of character. Integrity is everything. Without it, you have nothing.

What gifts do you bring?
PREPARATION
I'll help your customers get ahead of the curve. Around me, they'll feel prepared for what comes next.

CLARITY
I'll give your customers a sense of clarity. I'll help them apply logic and reason to any situation in order to see the best way forward.

EMPOWERMENT
I help people feel in command of their lives. In my presence, your customers will feel empowered to achieve what they most desire.

ASSURANCE
With my impeccable standards, your customers will feel sure they're getting the highest quality out there. Everything I present is triple-checked and stamped with my prized seal of approval.

What's your style?
MY PERSONALITY
Straightforward. Analytical. Strategic.

MY WORDS
Smart. Sleek. Scientific. Goals. Innovation. Justice. Civilization. Architecture. Achievement. Law. Efficiency. Logic. Research. Leadership.

MY SYMBOLS
Owl. Scales. Crown of Laurels. Ships. Olive tree. Square. Day. City. Pillars. Ladder. Flag. Compass. Library.

MY COLORS
Black. Gray. Gold.

Who are your favorite icons?

RUTH BADER GINSBURG
Supreme Court Justice

WILMA MANKILLER
Principal Chief of the Cherokee Nation

SUZE ORMAN
Money Management Expert

AMAL CLOONEY
Human Rights Lawyer

ADA LOVELACE
Computing Visionary

TONI MORRISON
Writer

KATHRYN JANEWAY
Star Trek Captain

I don't say women's rights—
I say the constitutional
principle of the equal
citizenship stature of men
and women.

Ruth Bader Ginsburg

Who is in your constellation?

IHI, Tahitian Goddess of Wisdom

SESHAT, Egyptian Goddess of Knowledge and Record-Keeping

JUSTITIA, Roman Goddess of Justice

SNOTRA, Norse Goddess of Wisdom and Prudence

ZEUS THE GREAT, ATHENA'S COUNTERPART

ZEUS: I am the ruler god. I'm a provider, a leader, and a guardian. My power is pervasive. I command the sky itself.

I am committed to creating a strong and lasting legacy. When I do things, I do them on a grand scale.

I mean business. I know how to cultivate alliances and consolidate power. My steady hand is unshakeable. Whatever I touch is marked by greatness.

I am Zeus—the Great.

MY FAVORITE ICONS

ABRAHAM LINCOLN
United States President

HIAWATHA
Co-Founder of the Iroquois Confederacy

MY WORDS AND SYMBOLS

Law. Leadership. Authority. Power. Building. Strategy. Decisive. Legacy. Crown. King. Seal. Monument. Marble. Lion.

ATHENA & ZEUS
BRANDS

CHIEF

The private executive network empowers women to reach new levels of corporate leadership.

THE FEMALE QUOTIENT

The platform is out to change the equation for women in business, advancing equality and closing the current gender gaps in pay and beyond.

K18

The science-backed hair care brand focuses on the patented peptide in its formulations and repairing hair on a molecular level.

TED

Driven by the pursuit of knowledge, the organization welcomes experts at the top of their fields to share what they've learned with the world.

Athena Brand

Sallie Krawcheck

Co-Founder and CEO of Ellevest

Before starting Ellevest, a woman-focused financial platform, Sallie Krawcheck had a storied career on Wall Street, serving as CEO of Smith Barney, Meryll Lynch, and Sanford C. Bernstein. After leaving Wall Street, Sallie set out on a mission to close the investing gap and help women grow their wealth.

Ellevest launched in 2016. As of 2023, Ellevest has raised over $153 million in funding, and has $2 billion assets under management (AUM).

Thousands of hours of research delving into what women are looking for in a financial company shaped the way Ellevest both operates and communicates. Every key decision at Ellevest is driven by data. And every communication feels welcoming, feminine, and entirely accessible. At every turn, one feels that this is truly a company built by women, for women.

Kate McAndrew: You have been called "The most powerful woman on Wall Street." When you were transitioning to start a business, many people suggested you start a platform for women but, at first, you rejected that idea. What changed your mind?

Sallie Krawcheck: Realizing the scope of the problem. One morning I recognized that the retirement crisis is actually a woman's issue. The retirement shortfall we have in this country, which is significant and rarely gets talked about, is a gender issue.

I'm an analyst by nature and by training. So, the first recognition was seeing this insight through the data. The second recognition was understanding that some good part of the retirement shortfall is due to the gender investing gap.

I didn't know if the problem was solvable, but I did know that I had as good a chance as anyone else to solve it. I know a fair amount about investing. I had been on Wall Street. And so, I figured I could raise at least some capital to put together a team and run after it.

It did take a while for me to allow my preconceptions about building a "woman's business" to drop away. I had a belief that doing something for women was somehow junior varsity. Eventually, I'd been away from Wall Street long enough to let that belief go.

KM: Right, there's this idea that things for women are un-serious. What I love about the Ellevest brand is that it does feel serious, yet also approachable at the same time. How do you think about striking the balance between seriousness and accessibility?

SK: I think of our brand persona as being your older sister who works in the investing industry, or on Wall Street, and comes home for Thanksgiving. The meal's just finished and you've all had a little bit of wine. You start to ask your sister these questions about investing. The conversation feels very loose, very intimate and familiar. She's giving you the straight shot. She's not hiding behind "basis points," and "drawdown risk," and "standard deviations." She's your sister and you can completely trust her.

KM: How would you describe the mission of Ellevest, and what values guide you as a company?

SK: Our mission is to get more money into the hands of women. Everybody at Ellevest rallies around this. We love to say, "Nothing bad happens when women have more money." Put another way, only good things happen.

Our mission is so powerful and has such force that it naturally shapes our values. One of our key values is to put her at the center of everything we do. This is something everybody in the industry says, but we take it very seriously. It comes into play whenever we make a big decision.

Another value that is so important to me is that we treat each other with MRI, which means the Most Respectful Interpretation of what anybody has done or said. So, imagine you're cut off by another car in traffic. Rather than immediately thinking the person's a jerk, you offer the most respectful interpretation of that behavior. Perhaps they're rushing their child to the hospital or taking their sick pup to the vet. We come back to MRI again and again in terms of how we engage and receive each other.

KM: One of the phrases you use at Ellevest is—*Money is not just money. It's the power to live the lives that we want.* You paint this very clear picture of how women are subjected to a kind of gridlock of shame around money. Whether it's for spending too much on lattes or for daring to have too much money, which is seen as greedy. Tell me about that.

SK: In research, men have shown they associate money with power, strength, and independence. Women, on the other hand, associate money with loneliness, isolation, and uncertainty. There's no amount of money they make that they don't feel embarrassed about—whether it's too much or too little.

The media messages we receive in our patriarchal system are around how dumb we are and how it's all our fault. Men get very affirmative messages around money, and women get very disempowering ones about how we're buying the latte or having too many facials. So, we feel it's our fault when actually it's because a woman earns eighty cents to the white man's dollar. . . . Yet we internalize the idea that it's our fault, and it festers.

You may have heard my friend Reshma Saujani say that boys are taught to be brave and girls are taught to be perfect. When you talk to men about money, they'll often use a water analogy and describe money as a river that comes in and goes out. There's more, and then there's less, but there's always more. For women, money is a pond. It's stagnant. There's only so much and it's going down. That's the current backdrop.

KM: While 86 percent of financial planners on Wall Street are men, 100 percent of Ellevest financial analysts are women. This is a critical brand decision. Why is it important for women to have other women as coaches?

SK: When women have women financial advisors, they invest 11 percentage points more than with a male advisor. Given that the stock market has historically been upward trending, that means that if you've invested more, you've made more.

We also know that women overwhelmingly believe the industry was made for men and was not made with them in mind. Research shows that two thirds of women investors believe their wealth managers misunderstand their goals. The majority of financial advisors are men and the majority of women are unhappy. Whereas the majority of male clients are very happy. I love to say that there's perfect product-market fit between men and their financial advisors and no product market fit between women and their financial advisors.

As we've grown, our decision to have women financial advisors has been partly based on intuition as well as a desire to take what the broader industry is doing and flip it on its head.

KM: You closed a $53 million Series B in 2022, a very difficult time to raise growth capital. The majority of your cap table is owned by women. Did you seek out female venture capitalists (VCs) explicitly, or did they simply understand and feel compelled by your mission?

SK: By the time we got to Series B, we were struggling to raise money. I've seen other FinTech and WealthTech company pitch decks, and I can tell you our numbers are terrific, but the raise was going poorly. You know, women CEOs raise one out of ten thousand Series B FinTech venture dollars, which makes the 1–2 percent statistic for certain other Series A/Series B categories look like child's play.

We decided to switch the strategy. Instead of going to people who make these investments and trying to convince them of our view of the world, we pivoted toward people who share our view of the world and tried to convince them to invest. As soon as we made that change, our hit rate went way up.

A woman on the West Coast heard about the round through one of our existing investors and reached out to say she was obsessed with Ellevest and would love to be part of this. She said, "I can't afford your minimum, but what if I bring a bunch of my buddies and we invest together in a special purpose vehicle (SPV)? We'll count as one investor on your cap table." Well, that led to someone from within that SPV forming another SPV, and then another SPV, and that's how we raised the $53 million.

KM: If Ellevest is successful in its mission, how will the world be different in ten-to-twenty years?

SK: If women have more money, everything's better. Some smart ass will always say, "Women will spend it." Yep, we will. Did you see what happened with Taylor Swift, Beyoncé, and *Barbie* last summer? We spent our money. There's a multiplicative effect when women spend money. I was in Pittsburgh two days after Taylor Swift performed there and people had a pep in their step. The hotels had been filled, the bars had been filled, and the shops had been shopped in. When women have money, the economy gets bigger.

As the gender and racial wealth gaps close, society is by definition fairer and people aren't as angry. There's a correlation between the wealth gaps and the anger in the population. Also, communities are stronger. Research shows that women invest most of their money into their community. Men do not.

With more money in the hands of women, more businesses are going to be started. When you have money, you have the confidence to take on a little more risk. You're able to leave your job and start a business that helps other women and their families.

Politics will improve as well. Is it any coincidence that women make smaller political contributions than men by a similar margin to what they earn vs. men? That doesn't mean every woman needs to vote a certain way, but if we're better represented, the research tells us that public policy-making will be more family-oriented and focused on children. I suspect if there were more women in power, the world would be a little kinder.

 ELLEVEST

A new way to feel confident about your money

Strategize for the year ahead with a financial planner by your side.

- **Three calls with the same CFP® pro**, so you can adjust your strategies and check in when needed
- **Personalized resources and easy-to-follow next steps** to help you make progress between calls
- **12 months of unlimited email access**, so you have peace of mind that you're supported at all times

(Explore the package)

Have $500,000 or more to invest? Ellevest Private Wealth Management may be a better fit for you. Learn more

WHAT WE CAN WORK ON TOGETHER

 Building an emergency fund   Paying off debt   Retirement planning   Setting financial goals

ATHENA BRAND

Sali Christeson
Founder and CEO of Argent

After years of frustration searching for workwear that suited her as a banker, management consultant, and technology executive, Sali Christeson decided to solve the problem for herself. In 2016, she launched Argent, a women's workwear brand that makes functional work clothes with attitude. In their words, they are "creating a movement that's all about self-expression in and out of the workplace, versatility as a power move, and radical equality when it comes to paychecks, pockets, and everything in between."

Both Argent's clothes and brand initiatives are conceptualized to bolster women with self-assurance, empowerment, and propel their progress toward their goals. Argent has several retail locations and sells nationally via their ecommerce site. The company, headquartered in NYC, is making significant strides in transforming the workwear category and the lives of working women.

Kate McAndrew: What's the origin story of Argent?

Sali Christeson: I'm really the consumer for what we've been building at Argent. My background is in business. I started my career in banking then got my MBA with a focus on supply chain and operations. Most recently, I was working in the technology sector at Cisco Systems. Throughout all these experiences, it was very obvious to me that working women were an overlooked category when it comes to apparel. It was a personal pain point for me, as well as for my peers.

In 2015, I read a study showing how women are judged based on their appearance at work. The study quantified the impact of what you wear on your income over your lifetime. The impact is really significant. So, I decided to start a company to redefine what workwear looks like for women and offer new solutions from a product perspective.

KM: How would you describe Argent's brand mission?

SC: Our goal is to remove barriers for women and give them confidence at every touchpoint. Whether you're wearing Argent on stage, at a board meeting, or testifying before Congress, we want you to feel your best. When you feel great, you carry yourself differently.

This feeling is something we want to offer throughout every experience that women have with our brand. Each time she steps into our store, comes to our website, or receives our catalog, we want to make sure we're giving her the confidence to bring her best self into the world.

KM: It's funny, I've been thinking about my firm's big annual meeting this fall. Our investors will be flying in from around the world for two days of programming that I'm in charge of, and I've been asking myself, *What the hell am I going to wear?* As soon as I started seeing women whom I admire wearing Argent suits on Instagram, I thought, *I'm going to wear one of these suits. I'll look good and I'll feel like I'm fully in my power.* So, I think you're delivering on your mission!

I love how as a brand you focus on the idea of "Work Friends" and have brought together women like Katie Couric, Erica Chidi, and Kara Swisher to be ambassadors for Argent. How did you arrive at this concept and also choose these particular women to partner with?

SC: Our aim with Work Friends is to share stories about many different kinds of careers and to spotlight some women you know (like Katie Couric) and others who you may not know (yet). We're interested in fostering discussions about what various career paths can look like. We feature people across all kinds of industries, from sports agents to podcasters to government officials.

When I was growing up, I didn't see a wide variety of careers modeled. I think representation and visibility of many kinds of professions is important. Work Friends is not about any one individual. It's about bringing all these women together and seeing what magic comes from that.

KM: In French, Argent means "money." How did you decide on this name?

SC: It was a happy coincidence. My great-grandfather started a company in the early 1900s called Argent. I didn't know him, but I've read his letters and have been very inspired by him. Beyond my personal story, I think it's perfect that Argent means money because, as a company, we want to be a part of closing the gender pay gap and moving women toward pay equity.

Naming a brand is hard. We came up with a million names and filled so many whiteboards, but we kept coming back to Argent.

KM: I'm curious about Argent's approach to pantsuits. Can you tell us about that?

SC: Argent is probably best known for our pantsuits as they are so identifiable, but we offer a full suite of apparel, which includes everything from jeans and tees, to vests and dresses. From the pantsuit perspective, the fashion industry has a lot of women working in it but, as you move up the corporate ladder, it becomes predominantly male. A lot of decisions about women's apparel have been made by men, which has led to the "shrinking and pinking" of suiting.

Historically, suiting was not created with women in mind, and there has been so little innovation in the category. It has left much to be desired. When Argent launched in 2016, no one had done anything interesting with the pantsuit in terms of style or function. At that point, people weren't even putting color into suiting.

As women, we need to feel really good in what we're wearing, and we also need to be able to do actual work. I think the Argent pantsuits visually are a good representation of who we are as a brand. They're designed to be totally functional; you can get your hands dirty in our suits. They allow you to feel great and really focus on the work.

KM: Argent has this fantastic brand line: "Attitude, Meet Ambition." How did you get to that phrase?

SC: A really good copywriter. And it's a perfect fit for us. It really captures our essence. We both celebrate and encourage attitude and ambition as a brand. For us, it's not about putting more pressure on women to lean in and get to the corner office. A decade ago, that was the focus culturally, and I think that point of view is really exclusive and alienating. Women already have enough pressure. We're interested in celebrating the work women are doing and giving them the confidence to believe that whatever path they want to pursue is achievable.

KM: What is your personal ambition for Argent?

SC: Our aim is to exist as a resource for women and to continue to be part of these incredible career moments and milestones. I personally want to be part of chipping away at the patriarchy. Argent really is my Trojan horse for gender equity.

Sali Christeson,
Founder and CEO of Argent

03
YOUR BRAND
BLUEPRINT

YOUR BRAND BLUEPRINT

Now that you've met the goddesses, you're on your way to developing your brand blueprint. This is the essential document that will capture each key element of who your brand is and what you're all about.

It is similar to what some strategists call your "Brand Identity" or your "Brand DNA." We like to think of it as a blueprint, because once completed, it will serve as a map for everything you do on your brand moving forward.

The foundation of your brand blueprint is your goddess. She's the archetypal character who will guide and inspire every other aspect of your brand.

The next element is your heart. Your heart is what your brand cares most about in the world. It's why you do what you do every day. Ideally, your heart will convey the genuine passion that lives inside your organization.

The third element is your gift. Your gift is the kind of feeling you want to give your customers. It's the promise you're making to them about the experience they'll have with your brand.

And the final element is your style. Your style is everything your customers see, hear, taste, touch, and experience from your brand. It's how you talk as a brand and also, how you walk.

Once you know your goddess, your heart, your gift, and your style—you know your brand.

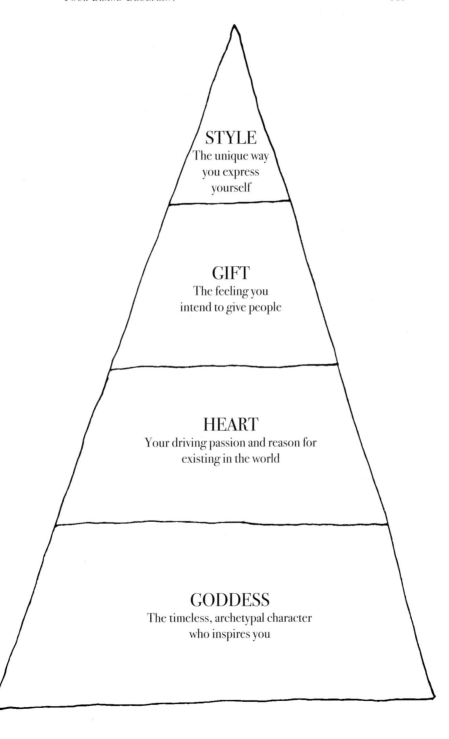

STYLE
The unique way
you express
yourself

GIFT
The feeling you
intend to give people

HEART
Your driving passion and reason for
existing in the world

GODDESS
The timeless, archetypal character
who inspires you

The step-by-step journey we're embarking on:

STEP 1
Finding Your
Goddess

Choose the archetypal goddess
to inspire your brand.

THE JOURNEY

STEP 2
Finding Your
Heart

Identify why you exist in the world
and the passion that drives you.

STEP 4
Finding Your Style

Explore how your brand lives in the
world; how you express yourself.

STEP 3
Finding Your Gift

Determine how you want people
to feel around your brand.

STEP 5
Your Brand Blueprint

Leave with a powerful map that will guide
everything you do on your brand
moving forward.

TIPS FOR THE TRIP

Before we get started, some considerations for making the most of this process:

Capture All Ideas

When an idea strikes, write it down! Be sure to capture all of your thinking as you go. At the back of the book, we've included an IDEA ORCHARD. It's a place to jot down your bounty of ideas that you can then pick from when the time is ripe.

Choose Your Own Adventure

Feel free to tailor the exercises to best fit your business context. If a prompt doesn't suit you, skip it! What's on offer here is meant to give you more than enough material to build your brand with.

Learn By Example

On p. 220, we walk through a case study that documents how a fictional company (Soft Scrubs Co.) conducts each exercise. As you build your brand blueprint, feel free to check out this sample case study. We created this in order to further illuminate the aim of each exercise.

Keep Moving

In this process, momentum is your friend. If you get hung up on a particular exercise, we suggest putting in a placeholder answer so that you can keep moving. Later, you can always return to it with fresh eyes.

Consider everything an experiment.

Corita Kent
Immaculate Heart College Art Department Rules

04
FINDING YOUR
GODDESS

FINDING YOUR GODDESS

Working with a goddess will help your brand exude the kind of magnetic energy that not only draws people toward you but also forges an emotional connection with them. This is essential. People make their decisions based on feeling first and reason second. Therefore, a powerful brand does both of these things:

CONJURES EMOTION
Appeals to the heart by inviting customers into a world that has a feeling and energy these folks are wanting to experience.

FORTIFIES WITH RATIONALE
Appeals to the mind by providing customers with material reasons that purchasing/subscribing makes good sense.

When your brand succeeds at both conjuring positive emotion and backing that up with strong rationale, you are guiding people on a journey to the kind of holistic, unabashed YES that leads to purchase (and retention).

Since both emotion and reason are important in branding, the right archetypal goddess for you is going to be one who both evokes an emotion your customers are wanting to experience as well as aligns with tangible attributes and benefits your product/service provides.

THE GODDESS EXERCISES

Through a series of exercises, you'll now uncover a number of possibilities for who your archetypal goddess might be. From there, a pressure test will help you narrow the field and make your final choice. You'll leave this chapter knowing your brand's goddess.

The reference sheet on the next page is intended to be a handy reminder of the goddesses we're working with.

This is a good moment to start a fresh notebook or virtual whiteboard to write down your ideas and responses to each exercise.

ATHENA
The Wise

VENUS
The Beauty

HERA
The Regal

THE GODDESSES

QUEEN
PERSEPHONE
The Fire

DIANA
The Free

HESTIA
The Sacred

DEMETER
The Love

MAIDEN
PERSEPHONE
The Dream

Every business situation is different. A few special considerations for the exercises, should they apply to you:

WHEN IT'S PERSONAL

If you will personally be the "face" for your brand, or its central representative among customers, then it's good to choose a goddess who is close to your own heart. In this case, have a look in the mirror and keep who you are in mind as you work through these exercises. Ultimately, you want to choose a goddess who you personally resonate with and feel is alive in you.

WHEN A GOD INTRIGUES

While our emphasis in this book is on the goddesses, the gods are also in play. If one of these goddess counterparts is intriguing to you, feel free to explore that in the exercises. We're referencing the goddess in our text, but know that you can definitely choose a god, or a goddess/god hybrid, as your brand's archetype.

WHEN YOU'RE AN ESTABLISHED BRAND

If your brand has been in the market for a while (be it years or decades), part of your task will be to determine how much (or how little) you want to evolve the core of who you are. Before jumping into these exercises, we suggest taking inventory of how customers currently feel about your brand. Dig into what they like most about you and why. Be wary of departing from these things! Instead, build on them.

Also, be aware of any negative sentiment that's out there. We don't suggest choosing a goddess who represents energies and attributes your brand has been historically weak on as this archetype won't feel credible to customers.

Goddess Exercise 1: The Natural

The purpose of our first exercise is to identify the goddess who is the most natural fit for your business category. Here, you're looking for the archetype who is connected in an obvious way to what you do as a company.

So, if your business is in the beauty category, the natural goddess for you will be Venus as she is the goddess of beauty.

If your business is in the outdoor apparel category, the natural goddess for you will be Diana as she is the goddess of the wilderness.

If your business is in the education space, the natural goddess for you will be Athena as she is the goddess of wisdom.

And if your business is in the cooking space, the natural goddess for you will be Demeter as she is the goddess of the harvest.

No need for this exercise to be a head scratcher. We're looking for your natural, automatic response here. First thought, best thought.

Who is the "natural" goddess for your business category?

Goddess Exercise 2: The Inspirational

In this exercise, the aim is to find the goddess who is most inspiring to you and your team. You'll be considering which goddess most excites you because of where she could help you take your brand. If more than one goddess is lighting a spark for you, that's fantastic. Write 'em all down!

Which goddess is inspiring you with a multitude of possibilities for how you could develop your brand?

Goddess Exercise 3:
The Match

Let's now explore which goddess will be a good match for your customers. You're looking for the goddess who your customers will be drawn to because she exudes an energy they want to feel and experience within the area of life your business serves. Think back to the party at the start of the book and consider: if all the goddesses were at the party, who would your customers want to talk with first?

To help with this exercise, we've created a handy Goddess Experience sheet (p. 154) that will help you think about the kind of energy each goddess is radiating at the party.

Which goddess (or two) will most appeal to your customer?

IMPORTANT NOTE!

If you already know a lot about who your customers are and what motivates them, then this exercise will be easy for you to do straight away. On the other hand, if you don't yet have a good sense of who your customers are and what they want, we've got you covered. Flip over to p. 230 at the end of the book. Here you'll find a Customer Toolbox waiting for you to open and work with. Once you've applied some of these customer tools and gotten to know your community better, you'll be ready to return to this exercise and complete it with confidence.

It doesn't always pay to be logical if everyone else is being logical.

Rory Sutherland
Alchemy

Goddess Exercise 4: The Unexpected

In this last exercise, you're searching for the goddess who can bring something different and even unexpected to your category. In branding, opportunity often lives in open spaces. Behaving in a surprising way can spark customers' curiosity and make your brand more memorable.

A great example of this is the water brand Liquid Death. Liquid Death channels the archetype of Hades–the Mystery. This brand character and style is so unusual and unexpected within the water category, you instantly notice it on the shelf. Liquid Death's counterintuitive, ultra-surprising archetype has been wildly successful.

To find the "white space" in your category, you'll first look to see what archetypes other brands are embodying. From there, you'll be able to tell where the unexpected territory is.

WHEN YOU'RE IN A CROWDED MARKET

If your company is playing in a crowded space, there may not be an "unexpected" archetype available. That is okay! Ultimately, your focus can be on expressing the energy of your chosen goddess in a way that is special and unique in your market.

_____

1. What are the top brands in your business category?

_____

2. Who are the goddess/god archetypes that these brands embody?

_____

3. Which goddesses would be unexpected in your space?

GODDESS EXPERIENCE REFERENCE SHEET

DIANA, THE FREE
FEELING
- Courageous
- Strong
- Capable
- Free
- Unlimited
- Wild
- Adventurous
- Fearless

EXPERIENCE
- Exploration
- Discovery
- Surprise
- Living for NOW

VENUS, THE BEAUTY
FEELING
- Worthy
- Inspired
- Decadent
- Indulgent
- Joyful
- Expressive
- Playful
- Sensual
- Fortunate
- Flirtatious
- Radiant

EXPERIENCE
- Pleasure
- Recreation
- Creativity
- Glamor
- Romance

DEMETER, THE LOVE
FEELING
- Nurtured
- Loved
- Abundant
- Secure
- Cozy
- Accepted
- Supported
- Understood

EXPERIENCE
- Comfort
- Compassion
- Bounty
- Safety
- Nourishment
- Warmth

MAIDEN PERSEPHONE, THE DREAM
FEELING
- Imaginative
- Youthful
- Optimistic
- Carefree
- Cosmic
- Open
- Rejuvenated

EXPERIENCE
- Sweetness
- Whimsy
- Magic
- Innocence
- Wonder
- Enchantment

QUEEN PERSEPHONE, THE FIRE

FEELING
- Passionate
- Fiery
- Provocative
- Irreverent
- Feisty
- Soulful
- Unconventional
- Unabashed
- Unashamed
- Bold
- Sexual

EXPERIENCE
- Revelation
- Transformation
- Change
- Intensity

HERA, THE REGAL

FEELING
- Elegant
- Established
- Classic
- Belonging
- Pulled Together
- Social
- Connected
- Tasteful
- Sophisticated
- Dignified
- Refined
- Fancy

EXPERIENCE
- Fellowship
- Camaraderie
- Tradition
- Hospitality

HESTIA, THE SACRED

FEELING
- Tranquil
- Calm
- Balanced
- In Flow
- Well
- Relaxed
- Soothed

EXPERIENCE
- Unity
- Peace
- Purity
- Healing
- Order
- Simplicity

ATHENA, THE WISE

FEELING
- Empowered
- Smart
- Intelligent
- Assured
- Clear
- Prepared
- Logical
- Rational
- Proficient
- In Command

EXPERIENCE
- Excellence
- Expertise
- Mastery
- Justice

CHOOSING YOUR GODDESS

Pressure Test

You've now unearthed many potential archetypes for your brand. The next step is to narrow the field and choose the best goddess for you. You're looking for the goddess who inhabits the sweet spot where who you are authentically as a company meets what is attractive and compelling to your customers.

To find the goddess who inhabits this sweet spot, compile a list of all the potential archetypes who emerged in Exercises #1–4. For each, consider:

Is she authentic?

Your goddess archetype needs to feel true to who you are as a company. If she doesn't, and you just don't see a natural connection to who you are and what you do, then she isn't the right goddess for you.

Is she attractive?

Your goddess needs to possess an energy that will be appealing and compelling to your customers. She has to inspire a feeling or experience they're wanting to have. Given all you know about your customers' motivations and desires, if you don't think she'll magnetize them, then she isn't a match for your brand.

Any goddess archetype who is both authentic to your company and attractive to your customers is a strong option for your brand. If several goddesses pass the pressure test, then the choice is yours. We suggest picking the goddess who you feel passionate about and who can ideally bring a refreshingly different energy to your category.

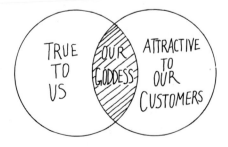

A brand becomes stronger when you narrow the focus.

Al Ries and Laura Ries,
The 22 Immutable Laws of Branding

1. Who are the goddesses that emerged in the exercises?

2. From this list, who is authentic to your company?

3. Who is also attractive to your customers?

PICK ONE

If in these exercises, you feel tempted to bring more than one goddess on board, we urge you instead to pick one. Why? Because brands benefit from focus. Focus is essential to crafting the bullseye brand transmissions that reach people easily and quickly and mean something to them.

As a reminder you can also choose one of the gods to be your archetype, or a goddess/god complementary pairing.

OUR BRAND BLUEPRINT

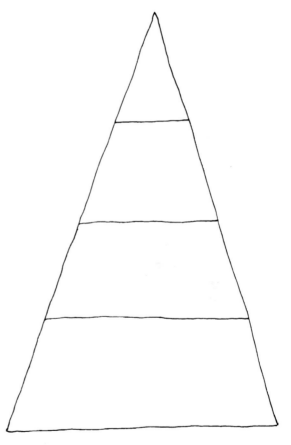

OUR GODDESS
The archetypal character who inspires our brand.

Congrats on finding your goddess! You're now ready to fill out the foundational layer of your brand blueprint.

05
FINDING YOUR HEART

FINDING YOUR HEART

Now that you know who your goddess is, the next step is to uncover the heart of your brand. Your heart is what matters most to you. It's the passion that drives you. It's why you do what you do every day.

A great brand heart will reflect a genuine feeling that lives within your company. It will be an idea that energizes you and moves you forward. It will also connect to the heart of your goddess, which will ensure that it can resonate deeply with your customer and touch *their* hearts.

THE HEART IS ACTIVE

When articulating the heart of your brand, we suggest using an active verb. The heart is always beating. It's never not in motion, just like your company. So, you want to write a statement that captures the mission you are on and the reason you are *actively* doing what you're doing.

THE HEART IS SIMPLE

You want to express your heart in a way that is simple and easy to understand. The brain is complex, but the heart boils things down to what's essential. With your heart, the aim is to write a clear, concise one-line statement that captures the passion that's at the center of everything you do.

The whats are important—they provide the tangible proof of the why—but the why must come first. The why provides the context for everything else.

Simon Sinek
Start With Why

CRYSTALLIZING YOUR WHY

Here are some examples of how a Maiden Persephone brand might take a rather complex, long-winded idea as a starting point and then crystallize that idea to create an elegant, meaningful heart statement.

THE COMPLEX IDEA	*THE HEART*
We believe that imagination is being stomped out by tech devices and so, we need to champion it at every turn.	Inspiring Imagination
It's our job to remind people of the inherent wonder in every speck of dust and every child's smile.	Spreading Childlike Wonder
There's a lot of negativity out there and when you're negative, you miss the true possibility that could be made manifest.	Seeing Possibility Where Others Don't

T he exercises in this chapter will lead you to several possibilities for your brand's heart. From there, a pressure test will help you define what matters most to you. You'll leave this chapter with a clear expression of the vital purpose that drives your brand.

Heart Exercise 1:
Personal Passion

In this exercise, you'll uncover your personal motivations for working at this company. If you're a founder, there's likely a compelling reason why you feel so passionate about the need for your company to exist in the world. And if you're a marketing professional, you can dive into all the reasons why you and your team personally feel good about showing up to work each day (beyond the money).

Write down everything that comes up!

Why are you passionate about this company?

Heart Exercise 2:
Heart of the Goddess

In this next exercise, your aim is to capture what your goddess cares most about. To answer this, you may want to jump back to Chapter 2 and re-read the interview with your goddess, particularly her response to "What's In Your Heart?" Keep in mind that what's shared there is simply a starting point. Use it as a launchpad for your own brainstorm.

What matters most to your goddess?

THE HEART EXERCISES

Heart Exercise 3: Core Convictions

This exercise will help you illuminate the core beliefs and principles that guide your company. Sometimes, the best way to uncover what matters most to you is to ask yourself what your business would never do. That answer can highlight what you feel strongly about and would never compromise on. From there, capture all the core convictions that drive how you operate.

1. What would your company never do? Why?

_____

2. What matters most to you as a company?

_____

L ook inside and see where the raw energy will come from.

Marty Neumeir
ZAG

CHOOSING YOUR HEART

PRESSURE TEST

A really good heart for your brand will be both true to your goddess and true to the genuine passion that lives within your company. That's the sweet spot we're going for.

Compile a list of all the active, simple heart statements that emerged in Exercises #1–3. For each, ask:

Is it genuine?

Your heart needs to reflect what you genuinely care about as a company. It needs to capture a mission and meaning that will inspire your whole team (and attract like-minded people to join you). If a heart statement doesn't feel genuine to your company or inspire a deep enthusiasm, ditch it.

Does your goddess care about it?

Your heart needs to be BIG. It needs to reach deep down into values and emotions that stir the soul of humanity. The best way to know if your heart goes that deep is to consider if it is close to the heart of your goddess. If it's not aligned with your archetype and something your goddess would deem truly meaningful, look elsewhere.

Any heart that rings true to your goddess and gives your team the sense that you're on a vital mission is a strong possibility for you. If many heart statements pass this pressure test, the choice is yours.

Keep in mind that there is likely going to be a whole set of values that are important to you as a company. These don't disappear when you choose your heart. What you're doing now is deciding what will lead your brand's expression. It's what you want to be known for.

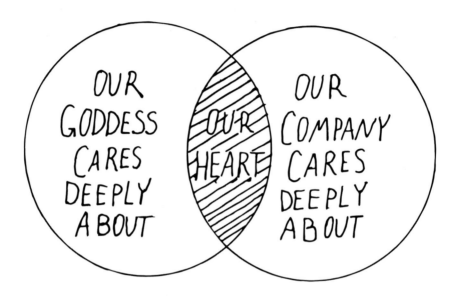

Make a list of all the potential brand hearts that emerged in the exercises.

For each, ask: Is it true to your company and inspiring to your team? Also, is it BIG and archetypal . . . can your goddess really rally behind it? If the answer to either of these questions is no, then it is not a solid choice for you.

OUR BRAND BLUEPRINT

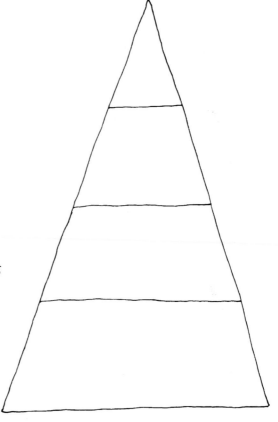

OUR HEART
Our driving passion
and reason for existing
in the world.

You have a heart! Now write it in the second layer of your brand blueprint.

THE HEART INTERVIEW
with Lori Boccato

Lori Boccato is a strategic consultant who helps brands define their purpose and then live it. Lori is passionate about framing opportunities and identifying solutions for businesses that are creating meaningful change in the world. She is managing director of Insights and Strategy at Global Prairie.

Jane McCarthy: Why is it important to get to the heart of your brand and clarify what matters most to you?

Lori Boccato: Most successful brands stand for something that is so clear and compelling that every single person who encounters them understands what they're about almost immediately. The best way to get to a clear, compelling brand identity is to find the core belief that deeply matters to you and really drives your organization. I think of this as articulating your purpose or why you exist in the world.

JM: How does articulating your purpose (or your heart) impact not just the experience customers have with your brand, but also the growth of your business?

LB: Many companies have a purpose that goes unspoken, and the people who work there seem to have a general understanding of what that is. I find that when a company decides to articulate why they're doing what they're doing, and actually write it down on paper, everyone in the organization can then rally behind it. The purpose becomes a guiding light that informs every company decision and helps to create a deep alignment between intent and action. It's a unifying force that drives consistency and keeps companies from diluting their brand as they grow and expand into new territories.

JM: Once you've articulated your purpose, is there a tactic you recommend for keeping this top of mind within your organization? It can be easy to lose sight of the big picture when you're in the mode of doing everyday business.

LB: At Global Prairie, we put the brand's purpose statement at the top of every brief. That way, it's the first thing everyone sees and, therefore, aligns to at the start of any meeting or review. It frames everyone's consciousness and becomes the filter through which ideas are evaluated and evolved. The purpose is placed at the top because it's the North Star. I think that's a simple, but very powerful way to reinforce and remind everyone of the mission.

JM: I love this idea. It highlights why it's so important to articulate your heart (or your purpose) in a way that is clear and concise. This way, it can be easily repeated and shared within your company. I'm curious, is there a brand you think does a really great job of living from the heart, if you will? Or put another way, is there an example of a brand where their purpose is clearly expressed in everything they do?

LB: Cuyana, the women's fashion and lifestyle brand, does a great job of this. Cuyana was founded by two women as almost an antidote to fast fashion. Their core statement, which I think reflects their purpose perfectly, is *Fewer, Better Things*. The clothes and accessories they make are expensive, but the idea is that the quality is so good, you only need one. So, you don't need forty sweaters. You just need this one, perfect Cuyana sweater that is super high quality, has a timeless design, and is going to last a decade.

I think Cuyana has grown like crazy over the past ten-plus years because they have such a clear core belief. Everything they do centers around this idea of *Fewer, Better Things*. They live up to this premise not only in their product design, but operationally as well. They were pioneers in bringing the farm-to-table concept to the fashion industry, and they share with customers how they source, for example, the wool for their sweaters in Scotland. They tell the stories of the heritage-driven (mostly) craftswomen who they work with around the world. Cuyana has also created their own resale market to encourage a more circular model. And then, their packaging and design aesthetic is very minimal. I think it's a nice example of how design can reinforce a purpose too. Cuyana genuinely cares about not being wasteful and as a customer you feel that in everything they do.

06
FINDING YOUR GIFT

N ow that you know who inspires you (your goddess) and what you care most about as a brand (your heart), the next step is to determine the positive, emotional impact you intend to make in people's lives (your gift).

An example of an iconic brand with a powerful, enduring gift is *Vogue*. *Vogue* is a Venus brand that at its heart, celebrates sublime beauty and creativity. It provides its community of readers a front row seat at fashion week and a seat at the table, listening in on what some of the most prolific creators of our time are thinking, feeling, and envisioning. At one level, the gift of the brand is that a woman anywhere, whether she's in a museum café in Milan or a roadside diner in Missoula, is going to feel an elevated sense of glamor in her life when she engages with *Vogue*.

If we venture even deeper, into the diamond core of the brand, the gift that lives there is a feeling of worthiness. The brand, at its best, is a reminder to women that they are worthy of this high fashion, this high art, this rich, abundant beauty—it is theirs every time they step into the world of *Vogue*.

With your brand, the aim is to identify the deepest, most meaningful gift you can give your customers. It will be meaningful because it is an experience or feeling they are wanting to have (whether they consciously know it or not). You also want your gift to be different from the kind of experience other brands in your category are offering. This is what will make it special and memorable for people. Finally, and vitally, your gift needs to be credible. You must be able to make good on your promise.

When you focus on giving your customers a gift that is meaningful, that is special, and that you can actually follow through on—voila!—you're in the realm of establishing trust. Trust is an essential ingredient for building a long-term relationship with customers and key to building a valuable business.

We humans are emotional creatures. We make our purchase decisions based on how products promise to make us feel.

Denise Lee Yohn,
What Great Brands Do

The reason people choose things 98% of the time is not rational. It's emotional.

Mike Cessario,
Founder of Liquid Death

Delivering a Feeling

When we talk about your brand gift, we want to be clear that we aren't referencing a physical product or a service you're providing; we're describing the feeling you want people to have during and after engaging with your brand in any way. Your gift is the emotional impact of your brand. Like being the lead singer of a band, your aim as a brand is to make your audience *feel* something.

The Gift Exercises

The exercises in this chapter will lead you to several possible brand gifts. From there, our pressure test will help you narrow the focus. You'll leave with a clear intention of how you want people to feel during and/or after an encounter with your brand.

The work you've already done to get to know your customer will be very helpful here, so be sure to revisit any and all customer learning as you move through these exercises. And if you find you need to do some additional customer research, consult the Customer Toolbox in the Supplemental section at the back of the book.

Gift Exercise 1: Legend

In most legendary stories, the heroine is faced with some kind of challenge that must be overcome in order for her to experience the victory she so deeply desires (and we, the reader, KNOW she deserves.) Often, at this precise moment of crisis, maybe when all hope is lost, a guide appears seemingly, miraculously, from out of the blue. This guide gives our heroine something—whether it's advice or a mystical talisman or a physical tool—and after receiving this gift, our heroine feels differently.

You are now going to write a legendary story of your own. It's going to be easy, because you'll be writing it Mad Libs-style. The purpose of your story is to think about how your heroine (your customer) feels before they interact with your brand, and then how they feel after. This "after" feeling is a good indication of what your brand gift could be.

(Fill in the spaces.)

At the start of our Legend, our heroine/ hero (i.e. your customer) needs or wants to _____ . The biggest problem in getting there is _____ . Goddess _____ appears before our heroine/hero, out of the blue, and shares our product/service/brand experience. It makes our heroine/hero feel

_____ .

The heroine/hero achieves what is desired and is crowned in a wreath of laurels.

I t's no accident that guides show up in almost every movie. Nearly every human being is looking for a guide (or guides) to help them win the day.

Donald Miller,
Building A StoryBrand

*Brands build strong
communities by ensuring
that everyone who takes
part in the brand feels like
an insider.*

Emily Heyward
Obsessed

Gift Exercise 2: From the Heart

In this exercise, you're going to capture the way the heart of your brand impacts your customers. The idea is to imagine how people will feel when they're around your brand as you beam out your heart energy.

Here is an example of a Diana brand heart and possible gift:

YOUR HEART   *YOUR GIFT*
    Inspiring Bravery in the   Confidence
    Face of Danger

_____

1. What is the heart of your brand?

_____

2. When you radiate your heart energy, how do people feel around your brand?

Gift Exercise 3: Brand Planet

In this last exercise, you're going to dig deep to discover the most powerful, positive emotion your brand can offer based on the material role you play in people's lives.

Imagine your brand is a planet. At the surface of your brand planet, there's what you do as a company. Just below the surface of your planet are the material (or functional) attributes of what you do. Beneath these functional attributes, there is a functional benefit of what you're providing. And beneath that, there are some common "everyday" emotions that your brand stirs in people. Then, finally, way down deep, beneath these everyday emotions are where our core feelings reside: emotions that are closer to the center of the human experience. These are the feelings that will be most powerful as brand gifts.

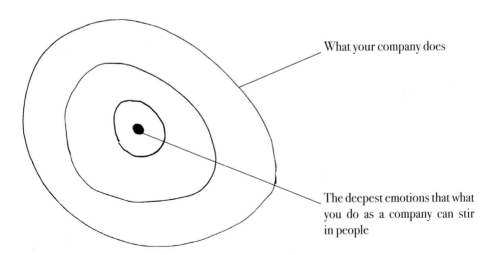

What your company does

The deepest emotions that what you do as a company can stir in people

1. What your company does:

_____

*2. The functional attributes of
what you do:*

_____

*3. The functional benefit of
what you do:*

_____

*4. The everyday emotions these
attributes and benefit spark:*

_____

*5. The deeper emotions that
stir beneath the every day:*

_____

CHOOSING YOUR GIFT

PRESSURE TEST

Now that you've found several potential gifts for your customers, it's time to pick one, wrap it up, and tie it with a bow. The perfect gift will be a feeling people are actually wanting to experience. It will also be special enough in your space that it motivates them to choose you over other options. Finally, it will be credible, given how you behave as a company. This is the sweet spot you're aiming for. Compile a list of all the gifts that emerged in Exercises #1–3. For each, consider:

Is it meaningful?

Is this gift a feeling your customers want to have in the area of their lives that your brand plays in? If the gift is not a feeling people want to have when they engage with your product or service, then it's a no-go.

Is it special or surprising?

Is this gift unique in your category? Will it motivate people to choose you over other options? If the gift is "table stakes" among everybody who offers the kind of product/ service you do, as in a basic feeling everyone is focused on providing, then it's not an optimal choice.

Is it credible?

Is this gift an emotion you can credibly deliver in your brand experience? Of course, you're not in charge or in control of other people's feelings (nor should you be) but generally, are their tangible ways your brand behaves that give people a chance to have this positive experience? If not, then the gift is simply not believable and could erode trust among your customers. In such a case, stay away. Better to play to your strengths.

Any gifts that are meaningful, special, and credible are all candidates. From there, we suggest choosing the gift that taps the deepest emotion. The deeper the feeling, the greater the power of your brand.

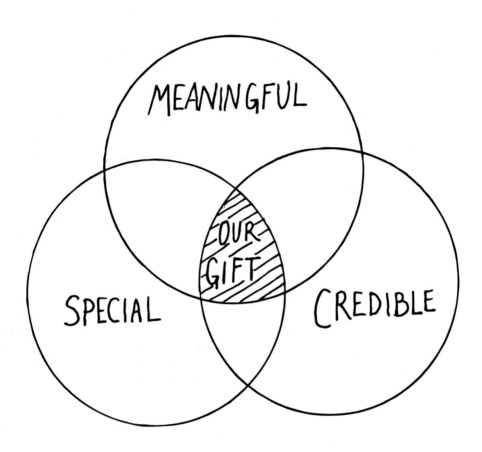

Make a list of all the potential brand gifts that emerged in the exercises. For each, ask—Is it meaningful? Is it special? And, is it credible?

OUR BRAND BLUEPRINT

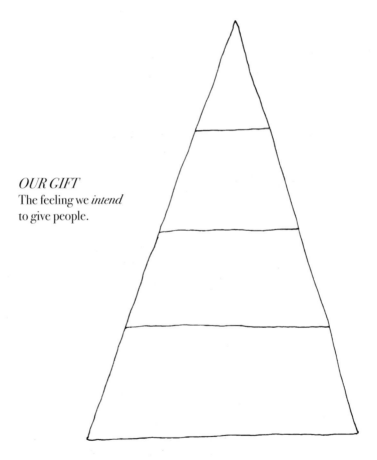

OUR GIFT
The feeling we *intend*
to give people.

You picked your gift! Now ink it in your brand blueprint.

THE GIFT INTERVIEW

with Katie Conway

Katie Conway is a brand builder who helps clients gain clarity on the promise they are making to their customers, then leads teams to design a brand experience that makes good on that promise. She believes that, in brand strategy, simplicity is your greatest ally. Katie is general manager at a global, brand-led experience firm.

Jane McCarthy: As a brand, why is it important to think about the kind of emotional impact you're making on your customers?

Katie Conway: We live in a world that is so noisy. It's nearly impossible to get someone to pause and pay attention, let alone remember you. When you need to build awareness for your brand, your best chance of creating a memorable impression is through emotion. People form memories around experiences where they really feel something. By infusing emotion into your brand, you're more likely to touch people on a level that will help them not only take notice but remember you beyond that moment.

JM: It's likely that customers are going to have all kinds of feelings and experiences around your brand. When you're in the brand-building process, why is it so important to focus on a specific "Gift" or kind of feeling you want to give people?

KC: When you try to be too many things to too many people, you end up meaning nothing to anyone. You have a vanilla brand that doesn't meaningfully connect with any group at all.

The strongest brands are just as clear about who they are not, and what they do not stand for, as they are about who they are and what they do stand for. Think about Southwest Airlines. As a brand, they stand for democratizing travel. That's the heart of who they are, and one way this shows up in their experience is that they have a single cabin. There's no first class vs. premium economy vs. economy. At Southwest, everyone is equal. Many people will never choose to fly Southwest because of this, and the airline is fine with that.

As a brand, you need to bring a ruthless focus and prioritization to what you're building. That's especially true if you're a new brand starting out in a crowded space. A singular focus will create a greater impact, and your dollar will go further.

JM: Once you know the specific gift you're intending to give people, how do you think about where in your brand experience to bake that feeling in?

KC: When you've decided to focus your brand on delivering a certain kind of emotional experience, you're making a promise to your customers that they will actually have that experience with you. Everything you do and say as a brand should be part of delivering on that promise.

That said, if you're inspiring powerful emotion at every single point along the customer's journey with you, that could be overwhelming. Instead, you want to choose two or three key moments where you really invest and provide a standout experience that evokes emotion and creates a lasting impression in people's minds and hearts.

JM: How do you recommend finding those two-to-three key moments to elevate?

KC: Identify where there are pain points in the standard customer experience within your category. Pain points are always opportunity zones for you to come in and transform what is usually something painful into something phenomenal, emotional, and, therefore, memorable.

Apple is a great example of a brand that recognized early on what a painful experience people had immediately after buying a tech product—and right when they were most excited to start using it! I remember getting paper cuts trying to pry packaging open. And setting up the new tech? Some of those manuals were pages and pages of jargon-filled gobbledegook.

Apple saw an opportunity to take a moment that was often filled with pain and frustration and transform it into a signature unboxing experience. The experience is beautiful, and the set-up process is so seamless; it makes it easy to start using your new product right away. That's an experience Apple over-invests in, in order to ignite customers' feelings of excitement and joy and, therefore, create a lasting impression.

07
FINDING YOUR STYLE

FINDING YOUR STYLE

You've now set the core intentions for your brand. You know the archetypal energy that is inspiring you (your goddess), you know what matters most to you as a brand (your heart), and you know the kind of feeling you intend to deliver your customers (your gift). The next step is to explore how you live these intentions in the world, and that brings us to style.

Your style is how you do what you do. It encompasses everything people will actually see, hear, touch, taste, and experience with your brand. It also includes how you show up operationally as an organization. In other words, your style is as much about how you walk as it is about how you talk.

We encourage you to cast off any ideas about your brand being an exterior coat of paint around your company, and instead see it as an ethos that is woven through everything you do—inside and out.

YOUR PLACE IN TIME AND SPACE

Your goddess is going to be a powerful ally as you develop your brand's style. She'll connect you to the universal language of symbol and story. The opportunity from there is to filter the timeless energies of your goddess into an expression that feels right for this time and the space your brand plays in it.

ICONIC + DYNAMIC

The expressions and actions of your brand are naturally going to evolve through time. There are, however, elements of your brand's style that you'll want to create and commit to as early as possible in the life of your company and keep beaming out far, far, far into the timestream. These key pieces of your style are what will make your brand iconic. It's what people will come to recognize and remember you by. These are your "always" actions and communications.

Then, there's the dynamic storytelling you'll do to keep things fresh, move with culture, and reflect what's

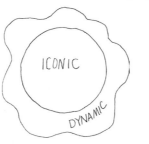

happening within your company. Dynamic storytelling is created in real time. For example, you might promote a limited edition flavor or work with influencers to create content around a timely event like Coachella. These are your dynamic actions and communications.

THE STYLE EXERCISES

The exercises in this chapter are focused on helping you develop the iconic elements of your style. These iconic elements are what you'll capture in your brand blueprint. We're also going to share some prompts to inspire ideas for your dynamic storytelling as well.

These exercises are a bit different from the ones we've shared previously. They are launch points for your own creative exploration. Give yourself, as David Lynch might say, "room to dream" here. Take your time. Trust that your desire for a breakthrough will lead you somewhere grand, and have fun with the process. We feel sure you will meet some glimmering and amazing ideas on your quest to create a living expression of your brand.

IF YOU'RE AN ESTABLISHED BRAND

If you're a brand who's been around for a while and you've already found a place in people's hearts and minds, part of what you'll be doing in the style exercises is thinking through which of your brand elements should remain, which should get refreshed, and which need to go. As much as possible, we suggest keeping the things people already love about your brand. Positive associations take time to build. Don't be too quick to ditch them in favor of the newfangled thing. Your existing brand equity is something to treasure.

Marketers can no longer use commercials to tell their stories. Instead they have to live them.

Seth Godin
All Marketers Tell Stories

Truly great communication—communication that creates, builds, and sustains the power of great brands—embodies an elementary paradox . . . It lies at the intersection of timelessness and timeliness. It captures or taps into a fundamental, enduring truth about the human condition. And, at the same time, it expresses that truth in a fresh and contemporary way.

Margaret Mark and Carol S. Pearson
The Hero and the Outlaw

Style Exercise 1: Your Symbols and Colors

In this exercise, you'll generate potential symbols and colors for your brand to own long term. You can start by making a list of the symbols and colors connected to your goddess and keep brainstorming from there.* Once you arrive at a short list, think about which ones will feel fresh or special in your category. Have fun experimenting with how you might weave these into both your brand's aesthetic and storytelling.

1. What symbols are connected to your archetypal goddess?

_____

2. What kinds of colors evoke the feelings you want to give people (your gift)?

_____

3. Of these lists, which symbols and colors would feel fresh or special in your category?

Style Exercise 2: Your Voice and Vocabulary

You're now going to craft how you talk as a brand. A great brand voice has personality. And so, one of the best ways to develop your voice is to consider the personality traits of your goddess. Once you've landed on your voice, the next step is to develop the beginning of a vocabulary you'll use to express who you are as a brand.

---

*   If your brand is communicating with an audience across several cultures, be sure to research the meaning of any possible symbols or colors with each group. Your style needs to convey the intention of your brand with cultural awareness.

A word or an image is symbolic when it implies something more than its obvious and immediate meaning.

Carl G. Jung
Man and His Symbols

Symbols are vessels for meaning . . . They are the fastest form of communication known to man.

Alina Wheeler
Designing Brand Identity

*Hog Island in the
Caribbean was going
nowhere until they
changed the name to
Paradise Island.*

Al Ries and Jack Trout
Positioning

1. What personality traits are connected to your goddess?

_____

*2. Of the list, what are 3–5 personality traits you'd like to
guide your brand voice?*

_____

*3. If you need a name, what are two hundred names you
could potentially call your company? (Once you have
your list, consult a trademark attorney!)*

_____

*4. What are some short phrases that perfectly express the
heart of your brand?*

_____

*5. What are some words you'd like to often use in your
communications? What words will you NEVER use?*

Style Exercise 3: Your Signature Experience

In theory, everything you do as a brand has the potential to impact your customers' experience and, therefore, the impression you make on them. In practice, you may want to choose certain areas to focus on that will be especially meaningful and memorable for people. In this exercise, you'll explore three areas (truly vast territories) where you might make a special impact.

---

1. How can your product, packaging, in-store, and/or digital experience give people the feeling you're intending to provide as a brand (your gift) in a way that is special and memorable?

---

2. How can you select your team and motivate them to exude the spirit that lives within the heart of your brand (especially those who directly interface with customers!)?

---

3. Who are some influencers and brands that are aligned with your ethos and could help you expand the impact you make on your customers through collaboration?

---

4. Are there any company practices/policies you currently have, or might introduce, that truly reflect the heart of your brand and are so special in your space that you could become known for them?

CHOOSING YOUR STYLE

PRESSURE TEST

You're now going to choose the iconic elements of your brand's style that you'll commit to beaming out through time. Take a look at all of the ideas that emerged in Exercises #1–3 and start picking out the pieces you love the most and feel you can truly make your own.

If you are able to invest in professional design help at this stage, we highly recommend it. On p. 236 you'll find a design brief you can fill out and share with your designer. And if you need suggestions for amazing women to work with, go to our site GoddessOffice.com where you'll find a Goddess Rolodex with phenomenal designers to consider.

Once you've arrived at what you think is a compelling set of style elements, ask:

Is it unique?

Is this style compelling and different in your brand space? Will it stand out in an appealing way?

Is it cohesive?

Do the pieces of this style work holistically? Together, do they create an overall expression of your brand that is greater than the sum of the parts?

When you've arrived at what will become your brand's signature style, etch these key pieces into your brand blueprint.

OUR BRAND BLUEPRINT

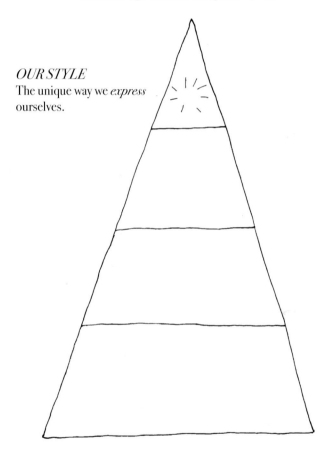

OUR STYLE
The unique way we *express* ourselves.

Magnifique! Everything you're doing, you're now doing with style.

THE STYLE INTERVIEWS:
SYMBOLS (AND MORE)

with Sarah Moffat

Over the past twenty-five years, Sarah Moffat has developed campaigns for some of the world's most iconic brands. Sarah is chief creative officer at Turner Duckworth where she leads creative teams for global clients such as Coca-Cola, McDonald's, Samsung, and Levi's. Her philosophy for getting to a breakthrough idea is twofold: stay infinitely curious and create from a place of joy.

Jane McCarthy: How do you think about symbols in your work?

Sarah Moffat: Symbols are essential in design. They help you connect with someone you've never met in a way that cues a deep emotion or even a memory. I use symbols instinctively and always like to explore how a symbol might behave in a way that's unexpected.

JM: Even though brands can now build whole, ever-changing worlds within the digital space, it's still important to have iconic brand elements that you own over time. What do you think are the enduring design assets a brand needs to have?

SM: On our team, we talk about needing to develop the hardware and the software of a brand. The hardware is sustaining. And then there's the software, which you'll need to change regularly to keep the brand ticking.

From a hardware perspective, you need to decide what your brand will be famous for. That is something to determine at the start of your journey. What that thing is, isn't always clear. Sometimes you need to spend a while creating and being open to where the energy is flowing.

My advice to anyone building a business is to be consistent. Brand equity isn't built overnight. We have a saying at Turner Duckworth: *Love the unmistakable.* Consistently elevate what you are already known for (or would like to be). And if what's unmistakable about you is starting to feel stale, find ways to put the familiar elements of your brand into a new context. Reframe them in some way, but don't abandon them.

JM: When you're developing creative ideas for a brand, how do you get inspired?

SM: I tend to go out and look for things in the real world. I like to go to exhibitions, but I'll go to the most unlikely places as well. Sometimes I love nothing more than to go to a grocery store in a rural town. I love seeing what's in there, how they're stocking the products and putting things together. That's as fascinating to me as an exhibition at MOMA. I'm always seeking the places where you wouldn't think inspiration would be hiding.

At our studio, compressed timelines mean that the easiest place to find inspiration is online. What's challenging about that is you never know how many people have also seen that particular image and nor do you know who truly created it. Downloading is not designing. When you copy and paste, you're not reaching for something that's truly ownable and unique.

What's powerful about going out into the world is that everything you experience gets filtered through you. You refine and build on the information you've taken in and the idea you then create becomes something special. So, instead of cruising social media, I suggest you go and do something completely off the wall.

Many years ago, I was working on a project for a company that made kitchen knives. A recent visit to a medieval castle became my inspiration. I was thinking about knights, dragons, horses, and things. Suddenly, I had the idea that if these guys were selling the sharpest knife, then it would be sharp enough to slay a dragon. That became the brand's symbol—a slain dragon—which was far more unexpected and intriguing than a traditional British crest.

The actual art of creativity, as opposed to just borrowing and perpetuating, is putting two things together to create something altogether new and unexpected. So, I suggest you try pulling from alternative realms that are seemingly unrelated to your brand and keep an eye out for the moment when suddenly, you've made it all make sense.

Finally, creativity should be fun. I'm not saying everything needs to be sunshine and roses, but you have to find the joy in what you're doing. I find that if there isn't any joy in the process, the result is never that great.

COLOR
with Laura Guido-Clark

Laura Guido-Clark has devoted her life to color. Her studio, LG-C Design, works with clients to bring color to products and environments. Laura's proprietary color system, LOVE GOOD COLOR®, is the first of its kind to define color's impact. Along with her own design practice, Laura hosts online training to help other creators master the fundamentals of color. In 2011, Laura founded the volunteer, nonprofit organization Project Color Corps™ to create change by painting underserved neighborhoods.

Jane McCarthy: Why is color so powerful?

Laura Guido-Clark: There's something about color that connects us all. It is a wavelength and it has the ability to speak without words. Color is emotional; it's deeply embedded in all of us.

JM: When you know the kind of feeling you want to give people (in our system, we call this *the gift*), how do you then go about choosing an appropriate color in order to have that effect?

LGC: Well, first, I want to dispel the myth that "color family" is the most important thing when considering a color's effect. It is only one dimension. It's really saturation and brightness that have a greater impact than the hue itself. It's the quality of the color that you need to consider in order to evoke specific emotions. For example, if you are trying to create a feeling of surprise or delight, you should dial up the brightness. Yes, psychologically, you want to think about what a color family does, but focusing on the quality of that color is vital.

JM: How do you approach color in relation to a product or environment? I'm particularly curious to learn how you think about the dynamic between color and texture.

LGC: In that case, it's good to understand whether you want your color to be refracting light or absorbing it. When you use a glossy finish, you're choosing something that will ultimately be bright, and shiny, and ultra-smooth. People will then experience the color coming toward them. A matte finish, on the other hand, will be more subtle. It will draw you in. There's a big difference in that feeling.

JM: Do you consider what's happening in the cultural context when you're exploring color choices?

LGC: I always choose color based on emotion as opposed to any kind of trend. But you do need to be aware of the symbolic meaning of color in relation to a particular culture overall. You need to be culturally aware and take time to understand the meaning behind colors for particular communities.

VOICE
with Myra El-Bayoumi

Myra El-Bayoumi builds, evolves, and sharpens global brands. She has more than a decade of experience crafting thoughtful foundations for both budding companies and bonafide corporations. A brand strategist by trade, Myra leads from concept to creative, guiding visual and verbal identity to make strategy tangible and meaningful.

Jane McCarthy: How do you distinguish between a brand's voice and its tone?

Myra El-Bayoumi: I think of your brand's voice as how your personality comes to life through language, and then your tone is how you modulate that voice within a certain context. So, let's say your brand voice is serious, stoic, and formal. Even then, on social, you're still going to be a little bit more casual and relaxed. And a brand whose voice is fun and lighthearted is still going to be a bit formal in a regulatory environment, for example. That's tone.

JM: Let's talk about naming. If you're an early stage founder and you've done the foundational strategic work for your brand (so, you know your archetype, your heart, and your gift), how do you suggest approaching the brand naming process?

ME: In a perfect world, I want to say that you take your archetype, your heart, and your gift and then you find the one word that symbolizes all of these things and miraculously, that name will also be short and easy to say in multiple languages.

In the reality of naming, things go differently. Your archetype, your heart, and your gift can be launch points for various creative avenues to explore. You want to be as expansive as possible with your name generation, going as far and wide as you can. Ideally, you'll have a variety of people in the room with varying levels of closeness to the actual business. You want people whose brains will work in different ways because they see the company from multiple vantage points.

Your aim is to draft several hundred names—maybe four or five hundred. From there, you'll cut the list down, but you're only looking to remove the ab-so-fucking-lutely-not's. Your new list will probably be hovering around two hundred names. At that point, you want to run your list through legal. I work with a wonderful trademark attorney who gives each name a grade based on the level of risk associated with it. Each name comes back with an A, B, C, or D grade. Ds are like, *You're going to be sued tomorrow*. Cs are medium risk, Bs are low risk, and As are no risk. It's very rare to get an A. I have seen an A maybe once or twice in my entire career. So, mostly you're working with Cs and hopefully some Bs. On a good day, your list of two hundred names will get cut down to ten-to-fifteen possible names with a B- or C-grade level of risk. If you have ten names to choose from, that's a lot.

With your short list, start "trying them on." Write each name on a sticky note and put it on your monitor. Try saying the word in the mirror. Ask yourself, *Could I actually wear this name and live with it? How does it feel in my body?* See if you can get to a YES.

JM: How can brands successfully foster dialogue with their community?

ME: Critical to this is giving the community real and meaningful access to the company—and to other members of the community. More than just responding to comments on social media or reviews online, it's about creating a safe and open space for congregation and ensuring the brand's leaders show up and authentically participate.

Gaming companies tend to do this really well. During my time working on Xbox, I saw firsthand the incredible access top influencers and diehard Xbox lovers had to the brand's leaders. Not only does that strengthen the consumer relationship with Xbox, but it gives the brand almost immediate feedback upon which to build, grow, and evolve. What makes that community so effective, in my view, is that the voices of all members are heard, valued, and listened to. The community is a team working together on strengthening something it loves, listening and learning in service of achieving a common goal.

WORLDBUILDING

with Ada Mayer

Ada Mayer is a creative director with extensive experience designing brands for emergent startups as well as evolving existing brands to increase relevance. Led by curiosity, Ada approaches brand development as a worldbuilder, as opposed to a creator of traditional, static "identities."

Jane McCarthy: As the digital space has expanded, brands are now building whole worlds. Can you share a bit about what brand "worldbuilding" means to you?

Ada Mayer: I like the word "world" because it's inherently experiential. It suggests you're inviting people into a space, rather than pushing out an "identity," which implies a façade. Branding used to be about pattern recognition with memorability being the goal. The market is now so saturated, you just can't cut through with a visual identity alone, no matter how good it is. What people remember are brand behaviors or experiences that have surprised, delighted, or touched them in some way that is personal.

    The opportunity now is for brands to be storytellers and to tell their stories in new and inventive ways. Brands need to be constantly iterating. A brand world is alive and in motion. A lot of world-building occurs, of course, on social, but it can also happen in retail, at events, on a website or through partnerships. There aren't any boundaries. It's about meeting your customers where they are, or inviting them to explore somewhere new.

    The hardest part about branding is choosing your focus, which is why archetypes are a great tool. Once you're clear on your core character, you can get truly dynamic in how that plays out in different spaces.

JM: For brands that have been around for years (or decades!), how do you approach shifting a brand's world either through an evolution or a full-scale rebrand?

AM: Usually, a company wants to do a rebrand because they are undergoing some kind of change and they want to communicate that to their customers. Often, the immediate assumption is to rethink the brand's visual identity. What's important to consider is how that reworking will meaningfully communicate the new state the company is shifting into. You don't want change just for change's sake. You want to change in a way that truly reflects your company's North Star.

Sometimes, a rebrand really isn't called for. I've had many conversations with clients where I tell them, "You don't need a rebrand; you need to expand the brand." Let's say a company has several new products. In that case, they may need to evolve their brand to encompass a broader portfolio, but that doesn't mean they have to throw everything out and start again. Instead, the question is how to add new parts that will bolster a strong foundation.

DIGITAL EXPERIENCE
with Rachael Yaeger

Rachael Yaeger is co-founder of Human NYC, a brand, design, and development shop focused on bringing warmth and humaneness to every project they touch. A natural entrepreneur, Rachael is also co-owner of the Roscoe Motel—a modest and clean fly fishing motel in upstate New York.

Kate McAndrew: What's your philosophy on creating a great digital experience?

Rachael Yaeger: We always say that a brand's digital store is its flagship store. It used to be that physical locations were paramount, but I think that's less and less the case.

At Human, when we're designing digital experiences, we don't typically build everything from scratch. We love Shopify and have found it enables us to create these beautiful, custom experiences for our clients and not break the bank doing it. With the birth of Shopify, a kind of "DTC playbook" developed that everyone has been following. There's been a standard of having a mini cart, fixed navigation, email pop-ups, etc. I think the opportunity now is to ask yourself, *What does my customer truly need and want?*

I always want to create a beautiful experience that is authentic and really impactful, but is also responsible, meaning that we can actually ship it.

KM: How do you like to be briefed by a client when you're creating a digital experience for their brand?

RY: The more a client knows about their brand, the more they avoid the exploratory work that tends to burn a ton of creative hours (and, therefore, cost a lot).

I love it when a client says, "We're obsessed with this Agnes Martin painting." Or, "We love these words from this poem." Coming to the table with a few really influential references is so helpful.

KM: Once you get to a minimum viable product, how do you think about optimizing and refreshing content?

RY: Websites are living, breathing things. Some of our clients get very focused on this moment of "going live." The important thing to remember is that you can always "go live" and then iterate. In digital, you can polish infinitely.

MATERIALITY
with Lauryn Menard

Lauryn Menard is co-founder and creative director of PROWL Studio, a design and material futures consultancy based in Oakland, CA. Lauryn's professional background spans the worlds of furniture, footwear, future forecasting, and material innovation. She brings all of this experience to bear when designing tangible, sustainable solutions for her clients at PROWL. Lauryn is also a professor of BioDesign in the MFA Design program at California College of the Arts.

Kate McAndrew: How do you think about the relationship between brand and product—and specifically, the materiality of a product?

Lauryn Menard: When a brand has a physical product, rather than just engaging people's vision and hearing, you're activating all their senses. Materials give people information about the energy of the brand, even if they can't make logical sense of it.

There are people who believe that when you use a product with materials that come directly from the earth, that gives you a certain energy. Think about being in a room made of stone, standing on a wooden floor, and touching wool. That is going to give you a completely different feeling than if you were walking through Target. Those two environments—the stone room and the Target store—are activating your senses in two very different ways. Both of these experiences are created by materials.

Materials are also a really important expression of values. For example, let's say you're a coffee company and all of your coffee is Fair Trade. You have high standards for the living conditions of the workers on the coffee farms, which is really important to you. In that case, when someone is opening a bag of your coffee, everything about that experience (not just the label) should reflect these values. When they pick up your bag, customers should be able to sense that you're Fair Trade before they even see the stamp.

KM: At PROWL, how do you approach working on product design?

LM: We like to begin with the end, which is the messy portion of a product's life. We like to paint the picture of what happens when that product no longer functions or isn't desired anymore. I'm in the camp that everyone should be concerned with sustainability and care about environmental impact as a basic standard. I don't think any product should be made out of virgin plastic at this point. So that is always important for any project we do. From there, the focus is on igniting the senses.

When I was working for a studio based in Vienna called Studio Riebenbauer, we did a pop-up in San Francisco called Cup of Ceremony. The space was a candle, tea, and ice cream shop—a full sensorial experience. I think this is what people are craving these days because they're spending so much time in the digital realm. It's another reason why extra care in the selection of materials is so important.

KM: Right, the materiality of things becomes more important when people are spending the majority of their day staring at screens . . . I'm curious, where do you see materials heading in the (near) future?

LM: I suspect we'll reach a place where we pass legislation that bans the use of virgin plastic in products. What that will mean is we'll have to mine for used plastics as a new resource, and this will lead to grinding existing plastic down to turn it back into a composite, leaving a lot of room to add things in. Brands could offset the carbon of their manufacturing by storing carbon in their products, effectively making them carbon neutral. With this approach, for example, it's totally possible to have a carbon neutral piece of hardware.

Another avenue that is ripe for exploration is the use of compostable materials. Right now, I'm working on a compostable shoe. It's similar to a clog and it has cinnamon in it. (*Lauryn holds up the shoe and sniffs it.*) When I talk about the senses, this is what I mean. This shoe is beautiful, it smells of cinnamon, and it can go into the dirt and break down after you're done with it.

You could put sage in this shoe, or eucalyptus. You could put a custom fragrance in this shoe. So, why not create multi-sensory experiences through the surprising use of materials?

EXPERIENCE
with Janet T. Planet

Janet T. Planet is an innovation and experience-designer who has worked with iconic, global brands like Disney and Virgin Voyages as well as startups in the early days of building. Janet's superpower is in creating brand experiences that forge a profound emotional connection with people while also driving businesses forward.

Jane McCarthy: When you're working with a brand that gets to create a physical environment for customers, how do you approach designing that experience?

Janet T. Planet: The first question I ask is, "How can I transform a guest from being an observer to a participant?" In any space, no matter how fancy the gadgets and contraptions you may have there, your greatest assets are hands down the people. I'm always looking for ways to encourage people to engage with one another, whether in a collective or in pairs, and to make the experience more interesting for each other.

Pulling someone out of their comfort zone a bit and inviting them to engage with others, that's very memorable. People call back these kinds of experiences. It's like, "I went to this place, and I met these interesting people, and we did this thing together." That's powerful, and I think that's why the work with Virgin Voyages has been so successful.

The whole approach with Virgin was to unlock the power of the people on the ship. And by that I mean, to design experiences that inspire people to collaborate instead of compete (like they do on most cruise lines—for reservations, show tickets, pool chairs, etc.) and to meet and experience one another. That's what makes it a magical trip. It's not the hardware onboard or the port destinations; it's the magic of the other people you're with.

JM: When it comes to Consumer Packaged Goods (CPGs), how do you think about creating a memorable experience for people, even though you're more limited than you are in a physical space?

JP: With consumer products, I always think the most important thing to consider first are the channels where you'll be delivering your product. Designing a package that looks great online can be very different from designing for a physical retail space. On-shelf, there are layers of discovery you can draw people in with—textures, scents, colors . . . it can be a real seduction. Something that plays well in a brick-and-mortar store, though, might not be as profound in the digital space. Online, you're thinking about how to call out to people often from a small mobile screen with tiny product images.

Another consideration for DTC products is the unboxing experience. People's expectations have been elevated in a monumental way, so, I think you need to deliver something really special in that opening moment.

JM: What's an example of a brand that has a particularly phenomenal packaging experience?

JP: I really like this DTC probiotics company called Seed. The probiotics arrive in this very beautiful box. It's kind of spell-binding—the textures and the thoughtfulness of it. And there's a message inside the box, *For your world within.*

SUSTAINABILITY

with Nichole Rouillac and Vicci Baigrie

Nichole Rouillac is the founder and creative director of *level*, an industrial design shop based in San Francisco. Nichole has deep experience taking complex new technologies and shaping them into forms that foster emotional connections between people and brands.

Vicci Baigrie is chief operating officer at *level*. Vicci has worked with the world's most influential and innovative companies supporting founders and designers in navigating the creative process.

Jane McCarthy: Even if you're not intending to focus on sustainability in your brand messaging, why is it still important for any brand with a physical product or environment to think about the sustainability of its practices?

Nichole Rouillac: I've personally spent way too much time at mass-production factories and have seen how devastating the practices at these facilities are for the planet. Tremendous waste, poisonous bi-products, terrible work conditions. In years to come, I think we'll look back at how the practices of many major brands impacted our Earth, and we'll view them in the same way we now view Big Tobacco. I recently went down a rabbit hole looking at old cigarette ads. It was astonishing to see doctors recommending cigarettes.

Vicci Baigrie: I do think we are soon going to see state, federal, and global mandates that require a variety of consumer goods companies to comply with certain sustainability practices. It's smart business to be ahead of the curve.

Kate McAndrew: What are some ways that aren't hugely capital intensive for brands to move toward greater sustainability?

NR: The easiest place to start is typically with your packaging. Most of the time, it's the product within the package that's the tougher, more costly thing to tackle. Going from a blister pack to a cardboard or paper box, that's a good start. Whatever you can do to remove any petroleum-based products—be it inks, films, or actual plastic packaging.

VB: Heath Ceramics is an example of a brand that does really inspiring work across the board and their packaging is no exception. They use ExpandOS' interlocking cardboard pieces, made from post-consumer chipboard, as filler, allowing them to safely ship a full dinner service—ceramic plates, cups, salad bowls—across the world without damage. It is inspiring to see such a popular lifestyle brand rethink standards in this way.

Ultimately though, we all need to recognize there is no "away." Wherever possible, consider using packaging materials that will naturally break down, whether people actually compost them or not. The composting infrastructure in most cities just isn't there yet, so materials that disintegrate on their own should be the target we all work toward.

KM: From a product standpoint, what trends are you seeing toward sustainability? I've personally been hearing a lot more about designing for circularity.

NR: We were doing a project recently around design-to-repair and came across the electric toothbrush brand Suri. They've designed their toothbrush so it can be easily opened and repaired. So, if your toothbrush breaks, you can send it back to Suri. They'll repair and refurbish it, then send it back to you. At the point when you decide you're ready to get rid of the toothbrush, it's 100 percent compostable.

It is important to consider parts and materials even as you sketch out initial concepts. There should be consideration for how many parts are needed, how they're coming together to enable access for repair, what materials are being used, and do these limit recyclability? These decisions affect form, function, and aesthetics.

JM: I'm curious, do you think it will become commonplace for brands to have Carbon Facts on the side of their packages the way we have Nutrition Facts on the back of food packs today? Will people come to expect to see these facts?

NR: I would love to see this. If Carbon Facts were ubiquitous, there'd be some real consumer shocks, just like when you go to order a milkshake at those spots that list calories! It would encourage us all to think twice about buying a disposable toilet brush, for instance.

This will take time because most companies don't even know that information themselves right now. You have to pay for a detailed Life-Cycle Analysis of your product and process, from manufacture to distribution and facilities. So, teams need to care enough to budget for it. It took a long time for Nutrition Facts to be mandated and for people to accept, understand, and use them. A lot of education was involved.

VB: It will happen to consumer brands and products. We are already seeing it in clothing with AllBirds and Pangaia, among others. B Corp Certification is an incredible platform celebrating those who are making change and holding companies accountable. It is becoming a corporate badge of honor. Ultimately, we as consumers hold the power—the more we ask for it, the quicker it will come.

COMMUNITY
with Sarah Hardy

Sarah Hardy is co-founder and COO of Bobbie. As COO, she leads internal and people operations. As an early employee at Airbnb, one of the fastest growing and most successful technology startups in history, Sarah has unparalleled experience in scaling people operations with thoughtful design at speed. Perhaps what makes Sarah most special, though, is the way she does this with a community-first attitude and an eye for inclusivity.

Kate McAndrew: At Bobbie, how do you think about building community?

Sarah Hardy: Our community is from the inside out, and it starts with our employees. We have a huge overlap of employees who are also Bobbie customers, and we intentionally blur the line between what it feels like to be a member of the Bobbie team as an employee and what it feels like to be out in the world as part of our community.

Before we launched, we got moms in a room who wanted to share their feeding stories. One mom was just out of the hospital and couldn't breastfeed. Another mom breastfed for eleven months and now had a kid who was saying her first words and starting to walk. It was eye-opening for us to see that our customers are in very different stages of the parenting journey and are having different experiences within those. We realized that the glue of our brand, then, is the feeling moms have within the Bobbie community. Our aim is to help them feel supported, whatever stage of the journey they're in. That's what binds it all together.

KM: Can you talk a little about your workforce?

SH: When the pandemic hit, we were just starting to hire people. We quickly realized that it didn't make sense to build a team locally in the San Francisco Bay Area and instead, we committed to being fully remote. Laura and I had both come from Airbnb where a big part of the company's success had to do with the way people collaborated in-person (I mean, it was a lot of stickies). So, choosing to go remote was a hard shift for us. We started asking ourselves, *What can the positive outcomes of this decision be?*

I was personally very jazzed to think about how we could build a truly diverse team by being remote. Our workforce at Bobbie is now made up of two-thirds parents. We're 90 percent women, 40 percent BIPOC, and our team lives in twenty-six different states. We could never have built this kind of team in the Bay Area, and we could never have afforded the caliber of talent we have on our team if we were paying Bay Area salaries. It was 100 percent the right decision for us.

KM: How do your internal company policies reflect the ethos of the broader Bobbie community?

SH: Human-centric design is table stakes now. In today's environment, you have to meet the needs of your team. If you're not, you're missing the mark.

During the pandemic, two-thirds of the people on our team gave birth. So, we had to work with a smaller number of people, and we had to reinvent what parental leave looked like. Many founders of startups take the perspective that they can't afford parental leave. I was like, "Fuck that." You know, we had to ask ourselves—*What are we building here, and how are we setting an example?*

We now offer something on par with many big tech companies. It's not on par in terms of paid time off (we aren't able to meet that), but how we facilitate the leave, how people feel when they go out, and how they're welcomed back, is thoughtfully designed. We spend time guiding managers on how to treat people, and we have a buddy system for when you come back. Our focus is always, "What do you need in this moment?" Oftentimes, what people need has less to do with facilitating the work and more to do with what's happening on the home front. I do think we set the bar for startups, and I'm proud of that.

CULTURE
with Elizabeth Barrutia

Elizabeth Barrutia is founder and CEO of BARÚ, a multicultural marketing agency based in Los Angeles that serves Fortune 500 companies as well as major nonprofit organizations such as Disney, FX, Del Real Foods, Fannie Mae, Covered California, and the California Department of Public Health. BARÚ helps brands communicate with cultural intelligence in order to establish a deeper connection within diverse communities.

Jane McCarthy: How would you describe the mission of BARÚ?

Elizabeth Barrutia: When we first started fifteen years ago, our tagline was: *Where multicultural meets the mainstream.* Now, here we are and 50 percent of the population is multicultural and is driving the zeitgeist of mainstream culture, be it in fashion, food, entertainment, or art. These demographic shifts have changed marketing as we know it, but a lot of corporations haven't caught up to that yet. At BARÚ, we're helping our clients craft inclusive marketing and media strategies from the start, through finding the universal truths that connect us all.

JM: We're in this exciting time where there's a lot of collaboration and intermingling of cultural influences. As a brand, how do you suggest approaching being innovative and creative within the multicultural context while not falling into appropriation?

EB: If something is culturally exploitative, it's usually extremely stereotypical. There have been times when brands have done that, and there's been a tremendous backlash. What you do as a brand needs to come from an authentic place that you can substantiate with your actions or brand attributes.

Having a broad range of perspectives in the room is important. The cultural intersectionality of our team at BARÚ definitely makes us stronger. A diverse team brings a variety of people who can use their own personal barometers to weigh in and help craft the most effective strategies.

JM: How do you approach "translating" a client's brand campaign for Spanish-speaking audiences? I'm curious how you think about the deeper translation of a brand's core idea as opposed to a more literal or surface translation of a campaign.

EB: It's never a literal translation. In order to truly connect with people, we can't simply translate marketing materials word-for-word. Instead, we look for how we can bring in cultural moments and build on existing cultural cues that people will resonate with. We think about diversity of representation and positive representation (which a lot of organizations are now doing and doing it well). And then, we do consider the language piece. Word choices can depend a lot on the audience we're speaking with. For example, we may use different words with a Cuban audience than we would with a Mexican audience (and so on). The voice also needs to be calibrated for the channel we're communicating in. For instance, the cultural cues for a social post may be totally different than they are for a thirty second national TV spot.

JM: How do you make sure you're getting the cultural cues right?

EB: It starts with the people on our team and our own lived experience of being Latino and Cross-Cultural. We bring a lot of intelligence to the table based on what we encounter in our daily lives. We also pay close attention to what is popping culturally in the community—in music, TV, food, etc. And then, we always recommend validating cultural insights through research with the consumer segment, be it syndicated, primary, or secondary research.

JM: Part of what you do every day is to help large, legacy corporations evolve in order to stay relevant. I'm curious if you have any advice for an entrepreneur who is just beginning their journey—in terms of thinking from a multicultural perspective from the start?

EB: First, look at what's going on in your own community. Culture is born at the local level. This is where trends emerge and take off. Having your pulse on several pockets of local culture is vital. And then, stay open and responsive. As culture moves and changes, try to always be ahead of the next trend that is emerging and about to take off.

ABUNDANCE
with Denise Beckles

Denise Beckles is an experienced chief financial officer, chief operating officer, and global strategist, with thirty-plus years of progressive experience in consumer goods and financial services. Denise has a proven record in delivering extremely positive outcomes in the mergers and acquisitions space. With both public and private company experience, Denise is an expert at driving successful annual operating plans, P&L, cash flows, and growth targets. Very few people truly understand and love both finance and brand the way that Denise does.

Kate McAndrew: How do you view the relationship between brand and finance?

Denise Beckles: The brand is the center of everything. Ultimately, it is the brand that lives and creates value. In fact, it is at the center of value creation. The numbers are an expression of the brand's strength. They represent how well the brand connects with consumers.

    I've always been a finance leader who believes that the only way for a company to be successful is to invest in its brands. As a CFO, I don't believe you can cut your way to success. I think brand is probably the first place to invest because you want to create such a strong connection with consumers that you can grow your product offerings and expand into new categories. You can leverage the relationship between the brand and consumers to generate profitability and growth.

KM: When it comes to acquisition and valuing a brand, what do you look for?

DB: When I'm evaluating a company, I don't just look at revenue growth. I actually look at the strength of the gross margin and the contribution margin in order to understand what kind of long-term potential there is. There are small brands whose revenue growth is somewhat limited by how much they can produce, but they're extremely profitable because they can command such high margins.

In that case, I'm interested in how engaged the consumer is with the brand. If people feel there is really something special about it, which comes down to the impact the brand is making on their lives—whether it's giving them a sense of tranquility, or of enjoyment, or conviviality with friends—the brand can charge a premium for its products. People will happily pay this premium because the experience they're having is so positive, and it's a feeling that is not easily replaced by another. Consumers who have an incredible affinity for a brand are not paying simply for the physical product itself; they are engaging in an idea that has meaning to them and inspires powerful emotion. It's all about the experience and connection.

KM: You've been a key player in stewarding a number of long-standing brands. What do you think it takes for a brand to endure?

DB: First, the way a brand stays alive is through financial performance. Financial performance, meaning, not just the P&L but also how solid and robust the balance sheet is and how much cash flow from operations you're generating. In my career, I have seen the importance of cash flow. When I joined General Electric, I managed their entire cash portfolio, which is probably about $10 billion moving around the globe daily. Through that role I came to understand the power of cash when you look at profitability.

When we talk about what will make a brand endure for hundreds of years, I think it's the capacity to evolve with culture and continue to breathe new life into its journey. I'm on the board of the King Arthur Baking Company, which is one of my favorite roles. The company was founded in 1790, so the brand is over two hundred years old. It carries the heritage and history of beginning when the United States first began. The people who were using King Arthur in the kitchen looked like me. They were servants and slaves.

Today, King Arthur is still used by African Americans but the brand tells a different story than it did when it first began. They focus on an inclusive, supportive baking moment that brings families together. The brand's tagline is *Let Good Things Rise*. King Arthur has changed with the changing landscape of the country.

KM: What one piece of advice would you give a new founder starting out on her journey?

DB: You need a great product, yes, but make sure the brand is what really resonates. Your brand needs to be able to stand on its own. I would honestly say if you have a hundred dollars, spend sixty of those dollars on your brand. People remember the taste of Coke because of the Coke brand. Not the other way around. Products come and go, but the brand is forever.

08
BON VOYAGING

Signed, sealed, delivered—it's yours!

Congratulations on your newly minted, hot-off-the-presses brand blueprint.

You've crafted a brand that is authentic to who you are, expresses the deep passion that exists within your company, and is poised to impact the lives of your customers in a way that is both positive and meaningful.

Now that you've created your brand blueprint, don't let it gather dust. This vital document is meant to be shared with your whole team. It will be especially useful at the moment you embark on a new project as well as when you're evaluating options and making decisions.

Your blueprint can serve as your North Star, guiding everything you do on your brand moving forward.

Bon Voyaging

As you begin to live your brand out in the world, remember to consistently share your iconic brand elements, weaving them throughout your storytelling. Beyond that, have all kinds of fun experimenting with new ways to be inspired by your goddess, live from your heart, and gift a phenomenal experience to your customers.

Pay close attention to what is sparking the most interest and enthusiasm in your community and do more of that. Go where the energy is flowing and ride that momentum.

If you ever find yourself in need of inspiration, you can always ask, "What would our goddess do?" She'll guide you. Bon voyaging and may your business prosper.

To every woman who generously shared your wisdom and experience in this book, thank you.

We are infinitely grateful.

Supplemental

FICTIONAL CASE STUDY

SOFT SCRUBS CO.

Our imaginary case study is about a direct-to-consumer apparel company that makes medical scrubs. A quick download about our startup:

OUR CORE CUSTOMER
Millennial Women Nurses

Our biggest opportunity is with millennial women nurses and so, we're building our brand with them in mind.

OUR PRODUCT DIFFERENTIATOR
Warm Inner Lining

Our scrubs are warmer and softer than standard scrubs. This is the functional attribute that sets us apart.

THE CATEGORY PLAYERS
Dickies and Figs

Dickies and Figs are the top brands in the market. Additional players include Jaanuu, Cherokee Medical Uniforms, Healing Hands, Infinity, HeartSoul, and Wink.

We'll soon be moving into production in downtown Los Angeles, but we haven't developed our brand at all. We don't even have a name. For now, our placeholder name is "Soft Scrubs Co."

We're excited to start building our brand blueprint and share our work as we go. Here's what unfolded when we did the exercises . . .

Goddess Exercise 1
Who is the "natural" goddess for your business category?

HESTIA, *THE SACRED*: Scrubs are worn by people whose job it is to heal others. Therefore, the goddess who rules wellness and healing is a natural fit.

Goddess Exercise 2
Which goddess most inspires you?

DEMETER, *THE LOVE*: We love Demeter's warmth and nurturing energy. This goddess is already giving us ideas about where we could take our brand.

Goddess Exercise 3
Which goddess (or two) will be most appealing to your customers?

HESTIA, *THE SACRED*: In our one-on-one interviews with nurses, we found that they are really craving calm and a sense of peace in their day-to-day lives and also, during shifts. Many people reported feeling stressed and anxious on the job (and outside of it, too). For this reason, we think Hestia, who radiates a feeling of serenity, would be very attractive to them.

DEMETER, *THE LOVE*: In speaking with nurses, we found that many felt burnt out from always caring for other people and not really being cared for themselves. Many not only had patients but young children at home too, so the demands for taking care of others really never stopped. For this reason, we feel Demeter who radiates a feeling of warmth and nurturing would be super appealing to these caregivers who sometimes need and want to be cared for themselves.

Goddess Exercise 4

1. What are the top scrubs brands and the archetypes they connect to?

DICKIES–Mars: Dickies focuses on endurance, everyday heroes, and getting real work done. The brand has a rugged, no-nonsense vibe.

FIGS–Venus: Figs is a fashion-forward brand that focuses on how good-looking its designs are. Symbolically, figs are aphrodisiacs.

JAANUU–Diana: Jaanuu is focused on peak performance and breaking through challenges.

CHEROKEE SCRUBS–Athena: The brand has a professional vibe focused on excellence.

HEALING HANDS–Hestia: The brand is focused on the healing role medical professionals play in people's lives.

INFINITY–Diana: Infinity feels like a fitness brand focused on action.

HEARTSOUL–Maiden Persephone: The brand is unabashedly sweet, bringing fairy dust to the scrubs category.

WINK SCRUBS–Maiden Persephone: The light-hearted brand focuses on how medical professionals work wonders.

2. Who are the goddesses that would be unexpected in your space?

DEMETER, *THE LOVE*
QUEEN PERSEPHONE, *THE FIRE*
HERA, *THE REGAL*

PRESSURE TEST

Finding Your Goddess

1. Who are the goddesses who emerged in the exercises?

> HESTIA, *THE SACRED*
> DEMETER, *THE LOVE*
> QUEEN PERSEPHONE, *THE FIRE*
> HERA, *THE REGAL*

2. From this big list, who is authentic to your company?

> HESTIA: We make scrubs for healers, which is authentically aligned with Hestia, who is the goddess of healing.

> DEMETER: Our scrubs are warm and soft, which is authentically aligned with Demeter, who offers a warm and compassionate presence.

3. From this smaller list, who is also attractive to your customers?

> HESTIA AND DEMETER: We think both of these goddesses would be appealing to our community. Hestia offers soothing and calm (which they want). Demeter connotes emotional warmth and comfort (which they also want).

OUR CHOICE

> DEMETER, *THE LOVE*
> We are choosing Demeter as our goddess. Not only is she the most inspiring goddess for us, but she is also unexpected in the scrubs category. We're thrilled about our choice!

SOFT SCRUBS CO.

Heart Exercise 1
Why are you passionate about this company?

Supporting nurses
Caring for the caregivers
Helping people who help our community the most
Working with family

Heart Exercise 2
What matters most to your goddess, Demeter, the Love?

Showing compassion to all
Protecting the vulnerable
Providing a bounty for all
Nurturing family time

Heart Exercise 3
1. What would your company never do?

Scrimp on the quality and excellence of our products
Let an employee fend for themselves in a time of need
Manufacture abroad

2. What matters most to you as a company?

Giving nurses the best
Taking care of our people
Supporting our local community

PRESSURE TEST
Finding Your Heart
1. What hearts emerged in the exercises?

Supporting nurses
Caring for the caregivers
Helping people who help our community the most
Working with family

Showing compassion to all
Protecting the vulnerable
Providing a bounty for all
Nurturing family time
Giving nurses the best
Taking care of our people
Supporting our local community

2. Which of these hearts are true to your goddess and genuine for your company?

We ruled out "Giving nurses the best" because it's more of an Athena heart statement.

We ruled out "Protecting the vulnerable," "Providing a bounty to all," "Showing compassion to all," and "Nurturing family time" because we don't think we can truly deliver on these promises as a company.

All of the other heart statements feel true to Demeter and authentic to our company.

OUR CHOICE

CARING FOR THE CAREGIVERS
We sparked to the idea of "Caring for the caregivers" as we feel very inspired to be giving care to people who are usually the ones providing support to others.

SOFT SCRUBS CO.

Gift Exercise 1: Legend

At the start of our Legend, our heroine/hero (i.e. your customer) needs or wants to <u>get through her shift feeling good</u>. The biggest problem in getting there is <u>exhaustion, burnout, and feelings of loneliness</u>. Goddess <u>Demeter, the love</u> appears before our heroine/hero, out of the blue, and shares our product/service/ brand experience. It makes our heroine/hero feel <u>comforted and taken care of</u>. The heroine/hero achieves what is desired and is crowned in a wreath of laurels.

Gift Exercise 2

When you come from your heart (Caring for the Caregivers), how do people feel?

Nurtured
Cared for
Protected

Gift Exercise 3

What emotions are at the core of your Brand Planet?

1. What your company does:
MAKES SCRUBS

2. The functional attributes of what you do:
SUPER SOFT, THICK INNER LINING

3. The functional benefit of what you do
WARM

4. The everyday emotions these attributes and benefit spark:
COZY/COZINESS

5. The deeper emotions that stir beneath the everyday:
COMFORTED AND HELD

PRESSURE TEST

Finding Your Gift

1. What gifts emerged in the exercises?

Comforted
Taken care of
Nurtured
Cared for
Protected
Held

2. Which of these gifts are meaningful, special, and credible?

All of them except "Protected." Our scrubs don't offer unique protection from potential harm, so we think this would be a confusing gift and not something that is credible.

OUR CHOICE
COMFORT
This idea came up twice in our exercises and feels deeply emotional, while also having a clear connection to the functional benefit of our scrubs. It's the perfect gift for our nurses!

Our Style Exercises: Recap

Our style exercises included some wild brainstorms and we left them with all kinds of ideas for what we could do on our brand. Our process really took off when we landed on our brand name: MOTHER SCRUBS. All of the rest of our iconic brand elements naturally flowed from there. We did a pressure test and found that most of our ideas were unique, because our archetype is different and unexpected for the scrubs category. And, we feel we've arrived at a signature style that tells a cohesive story. Our style:

SYMBOL
Heart

COLORS
Heart Red and Oceanic Turquoise (these colors inspire a sense of being swept into the heart and into a sparkling, warm ocean)

VOICE
Supportive, Warm, and Loving

WORDS
Name: Mother Scrubs
Phrases: You Are Loved. We Heart You. We Heart Nurses.

WORD BUFFET
Super Soft; Warm; Snuggly; Love

MORE
Texture: Super Soft

OUR BRAND BLUEPRINT
Soft Scrubs Co.

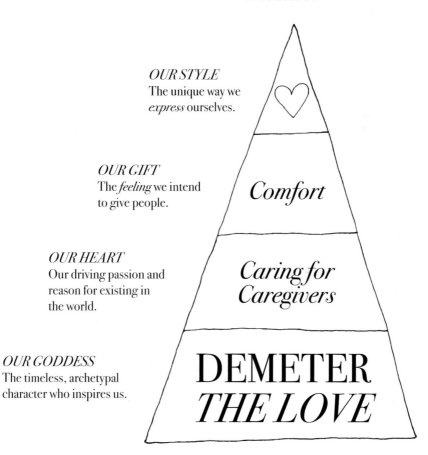

OUR STYLE
The unique way we *express* ourselves.

OUR GIFT
The *feeling* we intend to give people.

OUR HEART
Our driving passion and reason for existing in the world.

OUR GODDESS
The timeless, archetypal character who inspires us.

Comfort

Caring for Caregivers

DEMETER *THE LOVE*

YOUR CUSTOMER TOOLBOX

GETTING TO KNOW YOUR CUSTOMER

If you need to gain insight about your core customer group, this toolbox is for you!

There are a variety of ways to learn about your customers, and we recommend using as many of these as you can. Each approach has the potential to show you a new aspect of who your customers are and how they relate to your category. Some can be done from your phone and desktop. Others require you to do some field research. Each of these modalities builds to the final method in the toolbox—creating your customer portrait.

Your customer portrait incorporates all of the learning you've done on your customer and synthesizes this knowledge into one, clear reference sheet that you can always return to (and update through time). This portrait is where you'll highlight the attributes and attitudes that unite your customers.

ASKING WHY

As you use the tools provided here, the most important question to ask is WHY?

If a customer has a strong preference for briefs over thongs, the question is why? What drives that preference? If a customer loves getting to build her own pizza vs. ordering a standard pizza item on the menu, why? If a customer is feeling stressed or anxious in her life, why?

Do your best to get to the bottom of why a customer feels or behaves in a certain way. Ideally, you'll get to talk directly with people and ask them, "Why, Why, Why?"

You're on a mission to go as deep as you can. Get to know your customer the way an old-fashioned pen pal would. A good pen pal always wants to hear about the ordinary stuff of life—how the weather has been and what happened at the trip to the grocery store that day, but then, she's even more interested to know the stirrings of her friend's soul. She wants to hear about her most closely held visions and her most brutal heartbreaks.

The key to unlocking the hearts of your customers and getting them to share who they are with you is a genuinely curious "WHY?"

KEY CUSTOMER QUESTIONS

Beyond the all-powerful question of WHY, here are some ideas for what to explore in your detective work:

- Are there any demographic attributes that are common to these folks (i.e. gender; age; ethnicity; region; income; education; profession)?
- Do these people share a common life-stage (i.e. "newly married'; "empty nester")?
- Do they share any interests or passions?
- Do they have any common challenges or struggles in their lives? What keeps them up at night?
- Do they have any common dreams or aspirations?
- Why are they coming to the product/service your company provides?
- When they're shopping for this kind of product/service, what matters most to them?
- Do they have any needs they can't seem to get met in your business category?
- Ideally, what kinds of experiences and feelings would they like to have when using the product/service your business provides?

Tool 1: Social Media Dive

On relevant social media channels and community threads, get to know your customers by scanning commentary on topics related to your category, popular brands within your space, and your own brand (if you're in market).

Tool 2: Customer Reviews

Look at reviews of popular brands in your space—as well as reviews of your own brand (if applicable).

Tool 3: Trend Reports and Articles

Review existing secondary research about your customer and category by industry professionals, consultants, and journalists. Keep an eye out for any transformations in culture, technology, and generational attitudes that might illuminate what's happening in the lives of your customers.

Tool 4: Customer Data

If you have existing company data you can learn from, see what it can teach you about your customers and what motivates them to engage with your brand as well as purchase (and repurchase).

Tool 5: On-The-Street Observation

Go out into the world and observe people's behavior within environments relevant to your business. Look and listen in to see how people behave, what they say, what seems to bring them joy, and where they have complaints.

Tool 6: One-On-One Interviews/ Focus Groups

Talking with people one-on-one or in a group setting can be incredibly valuable to get to the bottom of what really matters to them and start to uncover ways you might play a meaningful role in their lives.

Keep interviewing people until you start to hear clear patterns in what folks are telling you. This usually starts to happen when you've spoken with about fifteen people. If you have a very broad set of customers, you may need to talk to more like forty people before you start hearing the similar things that illuminate patterns in how people are thinking and feeling.

Tool 7: Customer Survey

In an ideal situation, you can use Tool #6 to start to build some ideas and hypotheses about your customers and then you can validate these ideas with a larger group via a survey. The minimum number of respondents for a survey that is statistically relevant is usually somewhere around four hundred people, but any size can still be helpful.

It's always interesting to include some open-ended questions (along with close-ended, multiple choice Qs). Common words in these responses can make for word clouds that tell a powerful story about what's happening with your customers.

Tool 8: Customer Portrait

Building your customer portrait is a way to organize everything you've discovered about your customer into one simple framework. Here you're capturing broad information about the lives of your core customers as well as their attitudes and experiences specifically related to the context of your business.

On the following page, you'll find the template of a basic customer portrait. You can fill it out as-is or build your own portrait in a way that is tailored specifically to your company. The important thing is to include everything you think is essential to know about your customer.

CUSTOMER PORTRAIT

In Life Overall

Demo:

Life Stage:

Interests and Passions:

Dreams and Aspirations:

Struggles and Challenges:

In the Context of Our Business

Attributes/benefits that matter most when considering which brand to choose:

Desired Feelings and Experiences:

Frustrations and Struggles:

DESIGN BRIEF

Customer
Our core customer group is united by these things:

Archetype
We are inspired by:

Heart
We have a deep passion for:

Gift
The positive feeling we intend to give every customer:

DESIGN BRIEF

Iconic Elements
These pieces of our brand style are already "locked":

Creative Ideas
We have done a bit of our own brainstorming and are curious to explore:

NOTES ON THE GODDESSES

NOTES ON PERSEPHONE: MAIDEN/QUEEN

In myth, we first meet Persephone as a maiden. She is the very essence of youth. Sheltered by her mother Demeter, she is unaware of the difficulties of existence. She lives in a gauzy bubble, close to the magical realm of the nymphs.

Then, one day, everything changes. It is springtime and Persephone is frolicking in a sunny meadow, picking wildflowers. Suddenly, the earth begins to shake. The ground splits apart, revealing the mouth of the Underworld. Hades—the god of the Underworld—rides out of the depths pulled by a team of black stallions. He grabs Persephone, forcing her into his chariot. He absconds with her, taking her to his dark palace in the land of the dead. Persephone, the maiden, is imprisoned there, trapped in an eternal night.

The myth twists and turns. Demeter, Persephone's loving mother, will not let this abduction stand. She raises hell with the gods, forcing Zeus and Hermes to get involved and eventually, return Persephone safely to her, at Eleusis. But all is not well. While Persephone was in the clutches of Hades, she ate of his pomegranate seeds. She, therefore, must return to the Underworld for part of the year.

From here, the story splits. Maiden Persephone continues to live on in myth as the goddess of spring, the eternal youth, the symbol of renewal and all possibility. But she also lives a parallel life as Queen of the Underworld. And her character, as queen, is very different from her maiden form.

Christine Downing asserts, "The sexual symbolism (in the myth) is obvious—the radiantly awesome flower which Persephone reaches out to pluck as the earth opens up and Hades appears is clearly a phallus; the red-juice-dripping, seed-filled pomegranate which she eats in Hades suggests the womb . . . This "being taken" is in part being taken over by one's own capacity for passion; it is sexual ecstasy." *

Queen Persephone is resplendent in her full sexual power. She has eaten the seeds. She has known innocence, yes, but now she is experienced.

She has also seen some things most mortals (and even most goddesses) have not. The mysteries of life and

---

* Christine Downing, *The Goddess: Mythological Images of the Feminine* (New York: Continuum, 1981), 42–43.

of death have been revealed to her. As queen, Persephone then represents a deeper seeing, a deeper knowing. And to those with the courage to descend through the subterranean labyrinth and meet with her, a new—truer—vision.

Queen Persephone has transformed from the carefree maiden, unconscious even of the potential for danger, into she who has been initiated, she who has undergone the terrible trial, she who has been plunged to the depths of her own despair and risen up to take the throne that rules over the realm of souls.

The Persephone myth in its totality holds immense power in culture as it is an archetypal expression of the journey from innocence to experience as well as the heroic passage through the dark night of the soul where the heroine meets with death and is reborn anew. The wild popularity of The Twilight Saga by Stephanie Meyer attests to this. The virginal maiden meets with the vampire and is forever changed.

With brands, though, it is almost always more useful to consider Maiden Persephone and Queen Persephone as distinct archetypes and work with one or the other. Brands benefit from an archetypal clarity and simplicity of heart. For this reason, we have presented the goddesses as two separate archetypes in the book. Generally, a Maiden Persephone brand is going to vary greatly both in essence and in style from a Queen Persephone brand and to mix them would create confusion.

Occasionally we do see a kind of "mash-up" approach where the heart of the brand evokes Queen Persephone but aesthetically, it is more reflective of the Maiden. Billie, which we spotlight in the book, is an example of this kind of brand. Another example is the fashion brand Dolls Kill, which at its heart is about going against the grain (Queen Persephone) yet aesthetically, it merges leather and spikes (Queen Persephone) with coquettish, fairy-core elements (Maiden Persephone).

If you are considering a "blend" of the two Persephone archetypes, know that it definitely can be done but we recommend choosing one Persephone to lead and the other to show up primarily from a style perspective.

NOTES ON HERA

Many of us are familiar with the portrayal of Hera as a vengeful, jealous wife. Growing up, we didn't much care for Hera ourselves. Who would want to emulate such a venomous and spiteful goddess?

In myth, Hera is indeed seen as a "nagging" wife always "interfering and bothering" Zeus. And yet—as William Sherwood Fox points out—"despite all this, she is the "noblest of goddesses" and when she moves on her throne, tremors are felt throughout Olympus." Hera is "the Queen of all." She is the wife of the Pantheon. She demands a complete loyalty and allegiance. Anything less and Hera lets her displeasure be known. *

As Natalie Haynes illuminates in her book *Divine Might*, casting Hera as the villain in her marriage to Zeus (a known philanderer, to put it mildly) is patriarchal branding at its peak—"It is a misogynist narrative as old as time itself, and never out of fashion: the real problem in any bad family dynamic isn't the irascible, lecherous patriarch, but his patience-sapped wife." * *

In crafting our Hera archetype for this book, we have chosen to elevate the goddess's finest qualities—her interest in a deep and true partnership; her loyalty and sense of duty; her majestic aura that commands respect and awe from all; and how she holds court and negotiates various relationships with grace and aplomb. We have let the misogynistic narrative about Hera fall away. It may still be "in fashion" in certain corners, but we see no fruitful place for it in branding today.

---

* William Sherwood Fox, *The Mythology of All Races: Volume 1—Greek and Roman* (London: Marshall Jones Co., 1916), 164.
* * Natalie Haynes, *Divine Might: Goddesses in Greek Myth* (Great Britain: Harper Perennial, 2023), 51.

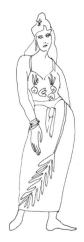

In myth, Venus arrives as a luminous vision, carried upon the crest of a wave. From the moment her toes touch down on speckled sand, her beauty leads gods and mortals alike into a rapture that artists have endeavored to express ever since. Few paintings are as indelible as Sandro Botticelli's *The Birth of Venus*.

While Venus, in mythology, is known as the goddess of beauty, of pleasure, and of desire, she is not, strictly speaking, the "goddess of creativity." She is, however, married (in a Venus sort of way) to Hephaestus, the divine smith. It is Hephaestus who creates Venus's golden girdle, part of her alluring and erotic costuming. Through this marriage, on a metaphorical level, we see how beauty and craftsmanship are inextricably linked.

Jean Shinoda Bolen observes that where the energy of the Aphrodite (Venus) archetype is present, so too is the creative force: "Creative work comes out of an intense and passionate involvement—almost as if with a lover, as one (the artist) interacts with the "other" to bring something new into being. This "other" may be a painting, a dance form, a musical composition, a sculpture, a poem or a manuscript, a new theory or invention, that for a time is all-absorbing and fascinating." * Bolen goes on to note that the creative process is very often sensual; it activates and impresses upon the senses.

In our characterization of Venus, we include her archetypal connection to creativity and to art. We give Venus some of the energy that in mythology was the domain of the Muses. This is useful for branding, because beauty and creativity are so deeply linked. Take Apple, for instance, an iconic brand that provides people with the best tools for creating. The beautiful design of Apple products is essential in the expression of its brand ethos. The same is true for so many brands—from Squarespace to Fender.

NOTES ON VENUS

---

* Jean Shinoda Bolen, *Goddesses in Everywoman: Powerful Archetypes in Women's Lives* (San Francisco: Harper & Row, 1984), 241.

NOTES ON ATHENA

Athena's mythological birth story unfolds in a peculiar manner. When Athena is still in her mother Metis's womb, her father Zeus hears that the child who Metis is carrying will one day rule the sky. Given that Zeus is the sky god, he cannot allow himself to be usurped. And so, he lures Metis into a game of his own devising, one where the goal is to become very small. Metis, ignorant of Zeus' intentions, starts to play the game, and she turns herself into an itty bitty fly. While she is in fly form, Zeus opens his mouth and swallows her whole. Metis, with her growing belly, becomes Zeus' prisoner, trapped inside his head.

Things go on like this until one day, Zeus suffers a terrible migraine. To relieve the pressure, Zeus has his head cracked open and out pops his daughter Athena. She is fully grown and ready for battle—adorned with shield, helmet, armor, and spear. From then on, Athena is very much her father's daughter. She follows Zeus closely; often does his bidding on the battlefield; and never acknowledges she even has a mother.

Unpacking this myth reveals some patriarchal dynamics at play. Here, the greatest masculine force around (Zeus, the sky god), tricks and degrades the very embodiment of feminine wisdom (Metis, which in Greek means "wisdom"). Zeus robs Metis, the mother, of her full procreative power, which was the heart of all cosmologies throughout the matriarchal age. Zeus essentially gives birth to his daughter himself. And this new daughter—born from the mind of the ruling man—is given the distinction of being the goddess of war.

Seeing the myth in this light makes us wonder if the "goddess of war" is a fabrication of the patriarchy rather than a deep truth of the archetypal feminine, expressed through story.

There is another famous myth about Athena, one that elevates a different aspect of her character. It concerns a time when both Athena and Poseidon are vying to become patron of the most important city in Greece. A contest is held between the god and goddess where each must present a gift to the people. Poseidon goes first. Raising his trident, he plunges it into the ground, which creates an earthquake. As the ground splits apart, up surges a saltwater spring for the people to bathe in. The gift is met with polite handclaps (keep in mind, these citizens live next to the sea).

Athena is up next. On the hill of the Acropolis, the goddess kneels and plants an olive tree, the first ever brought to the city. From the olive tree comes wood and from its fruit, olive oil. It's a gift that forever improves the lives of the people. Athena is immediately awarded the role of patron and the great city is given its name—Athens.

The founding myth of Athens illustrates Athena's distinct intelligence. How she is uniquely resourceful. How she strategically applies her brilliant mind. How she approaches real world problems with practical solutions that make a significant contribution to civilization.

Perhaps it is a lingering patriarchal patina on the image of this goddess that leads Athena to at times be characterized in our culture as being "masculine." And when her archetypal energy is expressed through the life of a woman, for that woman to then be described as being "in her masculine." Jean Shinoda Bolen clears up this confusion. She asserts that the traits of the goddess of wisdom, including logic, strategic thinking, and cool-headed, steady clarity, are absolutely feminine. When expressing these archetypal qualities, "Such a woman is being like Athena, not acting 'like a man.' Her masculine aspect, or animus, is not doing the thinking for her—she is thinking clearly and well for herself ... (this) challenges the Jungian premise that thinking is done for a woman by her masculine animus, which is presumed to be distinct from her feminine ego." *

Christine Downing suggests that the "re-membering of Athene (Athena) means the rediscovery of her relation to the feminine, to the mother, to Metis." * * In our system, this is how we are choosing to interpret Athena. As her mother's daughter. The goddess of wisdom by birthright, through the maternal line.

---

* Ibid, 78.
* * Downing, *The Goddess*, 117.

IDEA ORCHARD

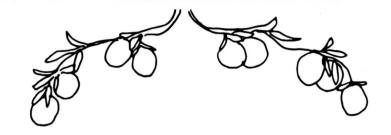

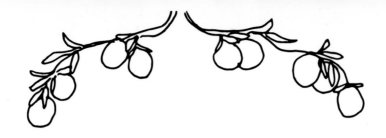

GOING FURTHER

SOURCES TO EXPLORE

If you would like to dive deeper into the world of archetypes, these books are a wonderful place to start. They are shared in descending order from the practical and mainstream to the esoteric and far-out. Choose your adventure!

The Hero and the Outlaw
Margaret Mark and Carol S. Pearson

Archetypes in Branding
Joshua C. Chen and Margaret Hartwell

Goddesses in Everywoman
Jean Shinoda Bolen

Divine Might
Natalie Haynes

Encyclopedia of Goddesses and Heroines
Patricia Monaghan

The Wisdom of the Enneagram
Don Richard Riso and Russ Hudson

The Inner Sky
Steven Forrest

The Way of the Tarot
Alejandro Jodorowksy and Marianne Costa

Asteroid Goddesses
Demetra George and Douglas Bloch

Angels and Archetypes
Carmen Boulter

REFERENCES

1. Demetra George & Douglas Bloch, *Asteroid Goddesses: The Mythology, Psychology and Astrology of the Re-emerging Feminine* (Lake Worth, FL: Ibis Press, 1986), 12.
2. Jean Shinoda Bolen, *Gods in Everyman: A New Psychology of Men's Lives & Loves* (New York: Harper & Row, 1989), 7.
3. Margaret Pott Hartwell and Joshua C. Chen, *Archetypes in Branding: A Toolkit For Creatives and Strategists* (New York: HOW Books, 2012), 11.
4. Debbie Millman, *Brand Thinking and Other Noble Pursuits* (New York: Allworth Press, 2011), 78.
5. Corita Kent, Immaculate Heart College Art Department Rules (1965–1968).
6. Rory Sutherland, *Alchemy: The Dark Art and Curious Science of Creating Magic in Brands, Business, and Life* (Boston: Mariner Books, 2019), 113.
7. Al Ries & Laura Ries, *The 22 Immutable Laws of Branding: How to Build a Product or Service into a World Class Brand* (New York: Harper Business, 1998), 8.
8. Simon Sinek, *Start With Why: How Great Leaders Inspire Everyone to Take Action* (New York: Portfolio/Penguin, 2009), 70.
9. Marty Neumeir, *ZAG: The Number-One Strategy of High-Performance Brands* (Berkeley, CA: New Riders, 2007), 49.
10. Denise Lee Yohn, *What Great Brands Do: The Seven Brand-Building Principles That Separate the Best From the Rest* (San Francisco: Jossey-Bass, 2014), 48.
11. Karen Heller, "Liquid Death is a mind-set. And also just canned water," *Washington Post*, June 17, 2023. www.washingtonpost.com/lifestyle/20 23/06/17/liquid-death-water-brand/.
12. Donald Miller, *Building a StoryBrand: Clarify Your Message So Customers Will Listen* (New York: HarperCollins Leadership, 2017), 32.
13. Emily Heyward, *Obsessed: Building a Brand People Love from Day One* (New York: Portfolio/Penguin, 2020), 94.
14. Seth Godin, *All Marketers Tell Stories: The Underground Classic That Explains How Marketing Really Works—and Why Authenticity Is the Best Marketing of All* (New York: Portfolio/Penguin, 2005), 26.
15. Margaret Mark & Carol S. Pearson, *The Hero and the Outlaw: Building Extraordinary Brands Through the Power of Archetypes* (New York: McGraw-Hill, 2001), 286.
16. Carl G. Jung, *Man and His Symbols* (Garden City, NY: Doubleday & Company, 1971), 20.
17. Alina Wheeler, *Designing Brand Identity: an essential guide for the whole branding team* (Hoboken, NJ: John Wiley & Sons, 2013), 32.
18. Al Ries & Jack Trout, *Positioning: The Battle For Your Mind* (New York: McGraw-Hill, 20th Anniversary Edition, 2001), 71.